RHYM

RHYME and REASON

John Metcalf and Gordon Callaghan

RYERSON EDUCATIONAL DIVISION
McGRAW-HILL COMPANY OF CANADA LIMITED

Toronto Montreal New York London Sydney Mexico
Düsseldorf Singapore Rio de Janeiro Kuala
Lumpur New Delhi

ISBN 0-7700-3211-7

17 18 19 20 21 22 23 24 BBM 0 9 8 7 6 5

PRINTED AND BOUND IN CANADA

ACKNOWLEDGMENTS

For permission to reprint copyrighted material, grateful acknowledgment is made to the following publishers, authors, and agents:

Abingdon Press for "New Snow" by Catherine Bryant Rowles from THE YEAR AROUND edited by Alice I. Hazeltine and Elva S. Smith, 1956.

Milton Acorn, for "Ghostly Story."

George Allen & Unwin Ltd., for "Hot Cake" from CHINESE POEMS by Arthur Waley.

Appleton-Century, for "The Flower-Fed Buffaloes" by Vachel Lindsay from GOING TO THE STARS. Copyright, 1926, by D. Appleton & Co. Copyright renewed, 1954, by Elizabeth C. Lindsay.

Barrie Books Ltd., for "To a Fat Lady Seen from a Train" by Frances Cornford from COLLECTED POEMS by Frances Cornford.

J. M. Dent & Sons Ltd., for "The Donkey" by G. K. Chesterton from THE WILD KNIGHT. J. M. Dent & Sons and the Trustees of the Dylan Thomas Estate, for "Mrs. Ogmore-Pritchard" and "Captain Cat" from UNDER MILK WOOD by Dylan Thomas.

Boni Liveright, for "Levy Silver" from THE NEW SPOON RIVER: Boni Liveright 1924.

Alan Brownjohn, for "After Prévert."

Jonathan Cape Ltd. and the Executors of the Lilian Bowes Lyon Estate, for "Early Light" by Lilian Bowes Lyon. Jonathan Cape. Ltd., for "Is It Far To Go" by Cecil Day Lewis from COLLECTED POEMS, 1954, The Hogarth Press Ltd., Jonathan Cape Ltd. and Mrs. H. M. Davies, for "Leisure" from THE COMPLETE POEMS OF W. H. DAVIES.

Chatto & Windus Ltd., for "Winter" by Richard Hughes from CONFESSIO JUVENIS. Chatto & Windus and Harold Owen, for "Dulce et Decorum Est" by Wilfred Owen.

Constable Publishers London, for "Flood" and "Plucking the Rushes" from 170 CHINESE POEMS, translated by Arthur Waley.

Doubleday & Company, Inc., for "Eight Haiku" from AN INTRODUCTION TO HAIKU, by Harold G. Henderson. Copyright © 1958 by Harold G. Henderson. Reprinted by permission of Doubleday & Company, Inc. For "A Green Lowland of Pianos" by Jerzy Harasymowiez from POSTWAR POLISH POETRY translated by Czeslaw Milosz. Copyright © 1965 by Czeslaw Milosz. Reprinted by permission of Doubleday & Company, Inc. For "The Heron" and "My Papa's Waltz," copyright 1942 by Hearst Magazines, Inc.

E. P. Dutton & Co., for "The Crayfish" from the book VIEWS FROM A FERRIS WHEEL by Robert Wallace. Copyright, ©, 1965, 1956 by Robert Wallace. (First published in the *New Yorker.*) Reprinted by permission of E. P. Dutton & Co., Inc.

Norma Millay Ellis, for "City Trees" from COLLECTED POEMS, Harper & Row. Copyright 1921, 1948 by Edna St. Vincent Millay. For "The Buck in the Snow" from COLLECTED POEMS, Harper & Row. Copyright 1928, 1955 by Edna St. Vincent Millay and Norma Millay Ellis.

The Estate of A. S. J. Tessimond, for "The Man in the Bowler Hat" by A. S. J. Tessimond.

Faber & Faber Ltd., for "Bombing Casualties in Spain" from COLLECTED POEMS by Herbert Read. For "Follower" from DEATH OF A NATURALIST by Seamus Heaney. For "My Parents Kept Me From Children Who Were Rough" from COLLECTED POEMS by Stephen Spender. For "O What Is That Sound?" from COLLECTED SHORTER POEMS 1927-1957 by W. H. Auden. For "Preludes (1)" from COLLECTED POEMS 1909-1962 by T. S. Eliot.

Farrar, Straus & Giroux, for "The Fish" from POEMS NORTH AND SOUTH by Elizabeth Bishop.

Samuel French, Inc., for "Moonlit Apples" by John Drinkwater.

Harcourt, Brace & World, Inc., for "Chanson Innocent." Copyright, 1923, 1951, by E. E. Cummings. Reprinted from his volume, POEMS 1923-1954, by permission of Harcourt, Brace & World, Inc.

Harper & Row, Publishers, for "Old Christmas" from LONESOME WATER by Roy Helton. Copyright 1930, by Harper & Brothers. Renewed 1958 by Roy Helton. Reprinted by permission of Harper & Row, Publishers.

Holt, Rinehart and Winston, Inc., for "Acquainted with the Night" from COMPLETE POEMS OF ROBERT FROST. Copyright 1928 by Holt, Rinehart and Winston, Inc. Copyright © 1956 by Robert Frost. Reprinted by permission of Holt, Rinehart and Winston, Inc., New York.

For "The Harbour" from CHICAGO POEMS by Carl Sandburg. Copyright 1916 by Holt, Rinehart and Winston, Inc. Copyright 1944 by Carl Sandburg. Reprinted by permission of Holt, Rinehart and Winston, Inc., New York.

Houghton Mifflin Company, for "The Garbage Truck" from "The Avenue Bearing the Initial of Christ into the New World" from WHAT A KINGDOM IT WAS by Galway Kinnell. Copyright © 1960 by Galway Kinnell. Reprinted by permission of the publisher, HOUGHTON MIFFLIN COMPANY. For "The Skaters" by John Gould Fletcher. For "Solitaire" by Amy Lowell from THE COMPLETE WORKS OF AMY LOWELL.

Hope Leresche & Steele, for "Goodbat Nightman" by Roger McGough from PENGUIN MODERN POETS 10.

The Literary Trustees of Walter de la Mare and The Society of Authors as their representative, for "All That's Past," "Autumn," "The Pool in the Rock" and "The Storm" by Walter de la Mare.

Macmillan & Co. Ltd., for "Mr. W. H. Davies" by J. C. Squire.

Macmillan & Co. Ltd., the Trustees of the Hardy Estate and The Macmillan Company of Canada Ltd., for "A Sheep Fair" and "Snow in the Suburbs" from COLLECTED POEMS OF THOMAS HARDY. The Macmillan Company, for "Factory Windows Are Always Broken" and "The Leaden-Eyed." Reprinted by permission of The Macmillan Company from COLLECTED POEMS by Vachel Lindsay. Copyright 1914 by The Macmillan Company, renewed 1942 by Elizabeth C. Lindsay. For "Cargoes" and "An Old Song Re-Sung." Reprinted with permission of The Macmillan Company from POEMS by John Masefield. Copyright 1912 by The Macmillan Company, renewed 1940 by John Masefield. For "Butch Weldy" from THE SPOON RIVER ANTHOLOGY: Macmillan 1914, 1942.

Macmillan Company of Canada and Mr. M. B. Yeats, for "Song of the Old Mother," "The Lamentation of the Old Pensioner" and "The Song of Wandering Aengus" from COLLECTED POEMS OF W. B. YEATS.

Methuen & Co. Ltd., and Clive Sansom, for "The Centurion" from THE WITNESSES AND OTHER POEMS by Clive Sansom.

Mrs. D. M. Mewton-Wood and W. J. Turner, for "Romance" by W. J. Turner from SELECTED POEMS 1916-36. Oxford University Press.

New Directions Publishing Corp., for "Two Children" by Nicolas Guillén, translated by H. R. Hays. Dudley Fitts, AN ANTHOLOGY OF CONTEMPORARY LATIN-AMERICAN POETRY. Copyright 1947 by New Directions. For "Six Variations" (#2) by Denise Levertov, THE JACOB'S LADDER. © 1960 by Denis Levertov Goodman. For "Yamabe No Akahito," poems #1, V, VI. Kenneth Rexroth, ONE HUNDRED POEMS FROM THE JAPANESE. All Rights Reserved. For "Deer" and "Lion" from "A Bestiary" by Kenneth Rexroth: COLLECTED SHORTER POEMS. © 1956 by New Directions Publishing Corporation. For "The Circus; Or One View of It" by Theodore Spencer, THE PARADOX IN THE CIRCLE. Copyright 1941 by New Directions. For "The Red Wheelbarrow," "Poem" and "This Is Just to Say" by William Carlos Williams, COLLECTED POEMS. Copyright 1938 by William Carlos Williams. All the above poems reprinted by permission of New Directions Publishing Corporation, New York City.

W. W. Norton, for "Like This Together." Reprinted from NECESSITIES OF LIFE, POEMS, 1962-1965 by Adrienne Rich. By permission of W. W. Norton & Company, Inc. Copyright © 1966 by W. W. Norton & Company, Inc.

Alden Nowlan and Contact Press, for "The Bull Moose" by Alden Nowlan. Robert Payne, for "Blue Is the Smoke of War" by Tu Fu, "Cold Mountain" and "Verses" by Wang Wei, "Death" and "The Evening Wind" by Lu Yu and "Verses" by Li Po from THE WHITE PONY by Robert Payne, The John Day Company.

Penguin Books Ltd., for "Alison," "Chanticleer," "The Miller," "Roger the Cook" and "The Summoner" from Nevill Coghill's translation of CHAUCER'S CANTERBURY TALES published by Penguin Books 1951.

A. D. Peters & Co., for "Mrs. Reece Laughs" from THE BIRD CATCHER AND OTHER POEMS by Martin Armstrong. Reprinted by permission of A. D. Peters & Co.

Laurence Pollinger Ltd. and the Estate of the Late Mrs. Frieda Lawrence, for "Giorno Dei Morte," "Mountain Lion," "Snake," "Things Made By Iron" and "Things Men Have Made" by D. H. Lawrence from THE COMPLETE POEMS OF D. H. LAWRENCE, William Heineman Ltd.

Queen's Printer, Ottawa, for "Autumn Baskets" by Miriam Waddington from "Call Them Canadians" produced by the National Film Board. Reprinted by permission of the Queen's Printer, Ottawa.

Random House, Inc., for "Auto Wreck" by Karl Shapiro. Copyright 1941 by Karl Shapiro. Reprinted from POEMS 1940-1953, by Karl Shapiro by permission of Random House, Inc.

James Reaney and Sybil Hutchinson, literary agent, for "Klaxon," from THE RED HEART by James Reaney.

The Ryerson Press, for "At the Lunch Counter," "Carl," "Fireweed," "The Fynch Cows," "Homebrew," "Saturday Night" and "Warren Pryor" from UNDER THE ICE by Alden Nowlan. Copyright 1961, The Ryerson Press.

For "The Flight of the Roller Coaster" from THE COLOUR OF THE TIMES by Raymond Souster. Copyright 1964, The Ryerson Press. For "Armadale Avenue Revisited" and "The Transformation" from TEN ELEPHANTS ON YONGE STREET. Copyright 1965, The Ryerson Press.

George Sassoon, for "Base Details" and "Counter-Attack" by Siegfried Sassoon.
Vernon Scannell, for "Cows in Red Pasture."

Miss Myfanwy Thomas, for "Digging" and "Tall Nettles" by Edward Thomas.
The University of Michigan Press, for "The Crabs" by Richmond Lattimore. Reprinted from SESTINA FOR A FAR-OFF SUMMER by Richmond Lattimore by permission of The University of Michigan Press.

Miss Anne Wolfe, for "Zoo" from CURSORY RHYMES by Humbert Wolfe.

Every reasonable precaution has been taken to trace the owners of copyrighted material and to make due acknowledgment. Any omissions will be gladly rectified in future editions.

INTRODUCTION

There are probably as many methods of teaching poetry as there are poetry teachers; no one method or teacher is infallible. We realize that this text reflects personal bias and that sections of the text may not please all teachers of English. However, most teachers would agree that the concepts explored in the text are fundamental to the understanding of poetry.

Although the lessons could be used as a complete poetry course, we assume that many teachers will use material from the lessons as a supplement to their own classroom teaching. The lessons were not designed to occupy single periods. Teachers may wish to add to or omit certain sections according to the needs of their classes.

All too often the technical terms and critical jargon of literary appreciation dominate the student's mind and prevent his responding to the power and importance of poetry. We have, therefore, deliberately simplified our terminology and concentrated on basic concepts.

Most of the poems in the anthology are modern. We feel that modern poetry has a more immediate impact on young students and helps to avoid the difficulties of archaic diction and unfamiliar attitudes. We hope that our selection of poems will introduce the student to ideas and feelings relevant to the world in which we live.

Gordon Callaghan
John Metcalf
Montreal 1968

CONTENTS

PART I

PART II

The Countryside

Animals

Pictures

Poems of Sorrow and Anger

PART ONE

Connotation

PLUS AND MINUS WORDS

CONNOTATION AND STATEMENT

CONNOTATION AND MOOD

CONNOTATION AND SOUND

PLUS AND MINUS WORDS

The doctor wrote *overweight* on Susan's card.
Anne said, "Susan's *fat.*"
Mary said, "Susan's rather *plump.*"

The words 'overweight,' 'fat,' and 'plump' are synonyms but do they mean exactly the same thing? Words, which are the building blocks of poetry, possess many subtle shades of meaning. Meanings are not fixed and constant; as you will see later, they depend upon context and usage. Consider the following words.

A. 1. If you were underweight, which would you most like to be called?
   a) skinny
   b) scrawny
   c) slim

2. If you refused to be drafted into the army, which would you most like to be called?
   a) a draft-dodger
   b) a traitor
   c) a conscientious objector

3. Which would an old man most like to be called?
   a) elderly
   b) an old man
   c) a dodderer

4. What is the difference between
   a) *stout* and *obese*?
   b) *slender* and *gaunt*?

Some of the words you have considered create pleasant and approving feelings and others unpleasant and disapproving feelings. If you react towards a word, whether approvingly or disapprovingly, the word is being used *connotatively*. If you feel nothing towards a word, it is being used *denotatively*.

B. In the following sentences the italicized words are being used in different contexts. Mark those used denotatively with a (o), those used with pleasant connotations with a (+), and those used with unpleasant connotations with a (−).

1. The scientists grafted branches onto the *immature* trees.
2. The prisoner named the other people in the *plot*.
3. My teacher is *ancient*.
4. The king often made *immature* decisions.
5. The teacher explained the *plot* of the novel.
6. The *ancient* buildings were carefully preserved.
7. Everyone admired the old man's *youthful* energy.
8. The doctors agreed that the child was *abnormal*.
9. His arguments showed too much *youthful* enthusiasm and not enough common sense.
10. There was no doubt that Peter was an *exceptional* child.

C. WORDS REVEAL FEELINGS

In each of the following sentences the italicized word causes us to respond approvingly or disapprovingly. Replace the italicized words with words or phrases which produce an opposite emotional effect.

Example: The soldiers quickly *retreated* could become: The soldiers *fled*.

1. The doctor had an extremely *self-confident* attitude.
2. John always ate *heartily*.
3. Mary *squandered* her money.

4. Alan read most of the time and the other students thought he was an *egghead.*
5. The old man saved a fortune by his *thrift.*
6. The *aroma* from the kitchen filled the house.
7. The saxophone *moaned* out the melody.
8. The neon signs *screamed* their messages at the shoppers.

D. BLITZKRIEG BANISHES BUGS

Nearly all advertisements rely heavily on the connotational use of words. The following paragraph is an advertisement for a cosmetic. See how many connotational uses of words you can find.

1. *Spring-time* is a miracle. A few droplets of dewy-moist *Spring-time* will smooth out those winter lines giving your face the pure bloom and young sparkle of Spring. See your face light up with the glow of sunshine. *Spring-time* is as natural as sunlight on the water of a stream. Don't delay. Breathe in the fragrance of *Spring-time* today—all the dew-fresh fragrance of the country in a slim, trim container to fit your purse.
2. Why are goods *on sale, reduced, reasonable,* but rarely *cheap*?
3. Why might an American whisky distiller call his product *Maclean's Loch Ness Choice Whisky*?
4. Why might a used-furniture store call itself *Ye Olde Furniture Shoppe*?
5. Using appropriately connotative words, invent a name for a bug-killer and write an advertisement for it.
6. Write an advertisement for a bar of soap, being as *soothing* as you can.
7. Invent a name and write an advertisement for a soft drink. (Stress how cold, sparkling, and refreshing the drink is.)
8. Why would *Stinko* be a bad name for a deodorant?
9. Why would manufacturers feel doubtful about calling a soap-powder *Scum*?

E. PLUS AND MINUS WORDS AT WORK

Read the following poem carefully.

CARGOES

Quinquireme of Nineveh from distant Ophir (1)
Rowing home to haven in sunny Palestine,
With a cargo of ivory,
And apes and peacocks, (2)
Sandalwood, cedarwood, and sweet white wine. (3)

Stately Spanish galleon coming from the Isthmus, (4)
Dipping through the Tropics by the palm-green shores,
With a cargo of diamonds,
Emeralds, amethysts,
Topazes, and cinnamon, and gold moidores. (5)

Dirty British coaster with a salt-caked smoke-stack
Butting through the Channel in the mad March days,
With a cargo of Tyne coal,
Road-rail, pig-lead, (6)
Firewood, iron-ware, and cheap tin-trays.

JOHN MASEFIELD

Notes

(1) *Quinquireme:* a ship rowed by five banks of oars.
Nineveh: a city in ancient Assyria.
Ophir: mentioned in the Bible as a land rich in gold.

(2) *apes:* a great rarity and curiosity in the ancient world.

(3) *sandalwood and cedarwood:* prized because of their beautiful smell.

(4) *Isthmus:* the Isthmus of Panama.

(5) *cinnamon:* a then valuable spice.
moidores: a gold coin of Portugal or Brazil.

(6) *pig-lead:* lead in pigs or blocks.

Verse One

1. In the first verse have the words 'home,' 'haven,' and 'sunny' pleasant or unpleasant connotations?
2. What is ivory? Is it valuable?
3. What sort of person would have owned 'apes' and 'peacocks'?
4. Sandalwood and cedarwood were precious because they were sweet-smelling. What do you imagine they might have been used for?
5. Think of one word to describe the cargo the ship is carrying.
6. From what period of time does the ship come?

Verse Two

7. In the second verse, have the words 'stately,' 'dipping,' and 'palm-green' pleasant or unpleasant connotations?
8. What is topaz? How many bright colours are suggested in the second verse?
9. Describe the cargo in a single word.
10. From what period of time does this ship come?

Verse Three

11. Select connotational words in the third verse. How do they differ from those in the first two?
12. Are there any words in the third stanza concerned with bright colour, taste, or smell?
13. A single word for the third cargo?
14. From what period of time does the ship come?
15. The cargoes of the first two ships are beautiful and luxurious while the cargo of the third ship is drab and merely useful. The first two ships are from ancient civilizations while the third ship is from our own. Do you think the poet is merely painting three pictures or is he, indirectly, passing an opinion? (Before you answer this question, think how the connotations of the words have made us *feel* towards the ships.)

CONNOTATION AND STATEMENT

Most good writers of fiction and poetry do not make direct statements in their writing. Statements do not affect our feelings. If Masefield had written, "I prefer the past to the present because the past was more beautiful," instead of writing the poem "Cargoes," you would not be reading his words today. If a poet wrote, "War is cruel and brutal," most people would agree and then forget his words in minutes. It is less easy to forget some of the poems about war you will read in this book. Writers of nonfiction usually make direct statements; poets usually show us pictures. They paint their pictures with connotationally powerful words so that the reader feels, understands, and draws his own conclusions.

A. THE CASE OF THE TRIPLE CHOICE

Imagine that you are writing the following paragraph from a thriller. Complete the paragraph by selecting from the three choices in each bracket that word which has the *most* unpleasant connotations.

> We turned off from the security of the main street with its bright lights and gay shop windows and plunged down a gloomy alley into another world. The buildings were black and (tumble-down, decayed, battered) and every window was shattered. Refuse (dirtied, littered, fouled) the streets and the (stench, odour, smell) was overpowering. At last, we reached the Rue Venida. Our guide stopped and looked (carefully, cautiously, furtively) about him. He then pointed to the doorway we needed and tucked the banknotes we gave him into the inside pocket of his (shabby, soiled, tattered) jacket. He (smiled, grimaced, leered) at us, showing his stained and broken teeth, and then seemed to melt into the shadows.

1. Although the writer makes no direct statement about the sort of man the guide was, we can guess fairly accurately. Which words and phrases suggest his appearance and personality?

2. From the feelings the connotations of the words have given you, what business do you imagine the men are going to conduct in the house?

B. THREE PICTURES

1. Miss Snettins clapped her hands briskly and glared severely at two boys who were still talking. Her hair was scraped back off her face and tied in a tight bun. Her cold eyes stared through rimless spectacles. She waited for a few seconds and then snapped, "Open your books at page seventeen."
   a) Has the writer made any direct statement which passes judgement on Miss Snettins?
   b) Does the writer like or dislike Miss Snettins?
   c) Which words in the paragraph enable you to answer the previous question? List them.
2. The cook slapped the steak down on a plate and then gouged a burnt spot out of it with his thumb nail. Then he shovelled on a scoop of French fries. He pressed the steak into place with his pink, sausage fingers, afterwards wiping them on his greasy, bulging apron.
   a) Has the writer made any direct statement which passes judgement on the cook or the cooking?
   b) Does the writer like or dislike the cook or the cooking?
   c) Which words in the paragraph enable you to answer the previous question?
   d) Which two words enable you to make a fair guess at the size and weight of the cook? What is the writer's attitude to the cook's size?
3. The old man worked on the length of wood with skilled and devoted hands. He worked patiently with his knife and chisel coaxing the graceful shape of the chair leg from the rough wood.
   a) Has the writer made any direct statement which passes judgement on the old man or his work?

b) Does the writer like or dislike the old man?

c) Which words enable you to answer the question?

C. PICTURE WRITING

As you have seen from your examination of "Cargoes" and the exercises you have just finished, writers make their statements in indirect ways—ways which not only give you denotational information but which also affect your feelings.

Select three subjects from the list below. Using the examples in the previous exercise as your guide, write brief descriptive paragraphs which convey an attitude without making direct statements. Your attitude to your subject, whether approving or disapproving, must be expressed by the connotations of your words.

a) an athlete
b) a politician
c) a cheerleader
d) a salesman
e) a pop singer
f) a disc-jockey

D. A VIEW OF THE CITY

Read the following poem carefully.

PRELUDE

The winter evening settles down
With smells of steaks in passageways.
Six o'clock.
The burnt-out ends of smoky days.
And now a gusty shower wraps
The grimy scraps
Of withered leaves about your feet
And newspapers from vacant lots;
The showers beat
On broken blinds and chimney-pots,
And at the corner of the street
A lonely cab-horse steams and stamps.
And then the lighting of the lamps.

T. S. ELIOT

1. What picture does the fourth line bring to your mind? Is it pleasant or unpleasant?
2. Think more closely about the words 'burnt-out.' What things become burnt-out? Is a burnt-out thing valuable?
3. Does the fourth line in any way change your reaction to the first three? Are the 'smells of steaks' to be thought of as pleasant or unpleasant?
4. Comment on the connotations of 'grimy,' 'scraps,' and 'withered.'
5. Can the word *vacant*—in 'vacant lots'—mean anything more than unoccupied?
6. Is the scene so far described an attractive one?
7. In the ninth line, what ideas does the word 'beat' suggest?
8. In what area of a city would the blinds be broken?
9. How exactly in the last three lines does Eliot convey a feeling of coldness and silence?
10. We start to read the poem as if it were purely descriptive but, when we finish a careful reading, we find that Eliot has moved us into an emotional attitude towards the scene. What do you think Eliot felt about our cities and the lives we lead in them?

E. Imagine that you are going to write a poem about a city as *you* know it. Think of the things *you* most dislike about that city. Make a short list of the details you would work into your poem.

CONNOTATION AND MOOD

From our study of the poems "Cargoes" and "Prelude" in the last two lessons, we saw that words used connotatively combine to produce a mood. The mood or feeling which a poem creates in us is a vital part of the poet's statement. The following exercises will enable you to explore further the creation of mood and to experiment with connotative usage.

A. Read the following lines carefully.

> The sun that brief December day
> Rose cheerless over hills of gray,
> And, darkly circled, gave at noon
> A sadder light than waning moon.

1. What mood do the lines create?
2. Which words create that mood?
3. What do the words 'darkly circled' suggest to you?

B. Reread the second verse of "Cargoes."

> Stately Spanish galleon coming from the Isthmus,
> Dipping through the Tropics by the palm-green shores,
> With a cargo of diamonds,
> Emeralds, amethysts,
> Topazes, and cinnamon, and gold moidores.

Explain how each of the following changes would be out of keeping with the mood which Masefield intended.

1. the substitution of 'ploughing' for 'dipping'
2. the substitution of 'tree-green shores' for 'palm-green shores'
3. the substitution of 'rock-sharp shores' for 'palm-green shores'
4. the substitution of 'uranium' for 'cinnamon'

C. The following verse about daffodils is from a poem by William Wordsworth.

> Continuous as the stars that shine
> And twinkle on the milky way,
> They stretch in never-ending line
> Along the margin of a bay:
> Ten thousand saw I at a glance
> Tossing their heads in sprightly dance.

1. Which words suggest movement?
2. If the poet wishes to convey a picture of the flowers waving in the breeze—a picture of their motion—why could he not have used the word 'march' instead of 'stretch' (1.3)?
3. What sort of mood does he create? Which words create that mood?
4. Would it make much difference to substitute a synonym such as 'blink' or 'flicker' for 'twinkle'?

D. Read carefully the following verse from a poem about winter.

Snow wind-whipt to ice
    Under a hard sun:
Stream-runnels curdled hoar
    Crackle, cannot run.

1. Which words convey harshness or coldness?
2. Which single word has connotations of pain?
3. Why is the word 'curdled' particularly appropriate?

E. This verse from a poem about winter also stresses the idea of painful cold.

The winter comes: the frozen rut
    Is bound with silver bars;
The snow-drift heaps against the hut,
    And night is pierced with stars.

1. Which phrase suggests that winter is like a prison? What do the words mean in a *literal* sense?
2. Which single word suggests the painful cold of winter?
3. Which word makes you realize that not only the natural world is 'bound' and 'pierced' by winter?

F. The following list contains words which are powerfully connotative. Consider the list until a descriptive idea is suggested to your imagination. Using words from the list and any other words you need to create your effect, write a descriptive paragraph which maintains a consistent mood.

1.

hover	shatter	gloom
prowl	muffled	dreary
slither	lurk	dank
screech	limp	stifle
moan	pierce	shuffle
glower	crawl	shadowy
threatening	looming	sombre
stealthy	slimy	

2. Write a similar descriptive paragraph maintaining a consistent mood. Let the words in the following list suggest an idea to you.

warm	swirling	glitter
ringing	quick	painted
carefree	silken	soar
glow	flashing	prance
gay	bounce	golden
splashing	lithe	skip
light	billowing	nimble
floating	graceful	sprightly

G. Many legends, fairy tales, and myths describe a hero going out to slay a monster. The following poem is a comical version of this type of story.

JABBERWOCKY

'Twas brillig, and the slithy toves
    Did gyre and gimble in the wabe:
All mimsy were the borogoves,
    And the mome raths outgrabe.

"Beware the Jabberwock, my son!
    The jaws that bite, the claws that catch!
Beware the Jubjub bird, and shun
    The frumious Bandersnatch!"

He took his vorpal sword in hand;
    Long time the manxome foe he sought—
So rested he by the Tumtum tree,
    And stood awhile in thought.

And, as in uffish thought he stood,
    The Jabberwock, with eyes of flame,
Came whiffling through the tulgey wood,
    And burbled as it came!

One, two! One, two! And through and through
    The vorpal blade went snicker-snack!
He left it dead, and with its head
    He went galumphing back.

"And hast thou slain the Jabberwock?
    Come to my arms, my beamish boy!
O frabjous day! Callooh, Callay!"
    He chortled in his joy.

'Twas brillig, and the slithy toves
    Did gyre and gimble in the wabe:
All mimsy were the borogoves,
    And the mome raths outgrabe.

The first verse sets the mood for the story. Father and son seem to be standing by the side of a lake or swamp where peculiar and threatening creatures live while the father is giving instructions before the son sets out on his quest to destroy the Jabberwock.

Many of the words the poet uses are made up of two or more words compressed to form a new word. 'Slithy,' for example, is probably made up of 'lithe' and 'slimy.'

1. a) What do you imagine a 'tove' to be? Is it pleasant or unpleasant?
   b) What might 'raths' be? Pleasant or unpleasant sounding?

c) 'Outgrabe' seems to be a verb. What sort of action do you feel it to be?

d) Can you find two words which seem to make the 'slithy toves' less threatening?

2. What connotations do the words 'uffish,' 'galumphing,' and 'beamish' suggest to you? Do you think that the hero in the poem is typical of the heroes in romantic stories?
3. Is the Jabberwock a fearsome animal? Consider the connotations of 'whiffling,' 'burbled,' and 'manxome.'
4. Was the battle between the hero and the Jabberwock a desperate affair? How can you tell?

CONNOTATION AND SOUND

Many words sound like the object or action they represent. At a very obvious level, such words as 'crash' and 'crack' imitate the sound of something breaking or snapping. But the relationship between sound and meaning can be less obvious. Words such as 'stab,' 'soft,' and 'soothing' retain elements of imitation but these elements are much more subtle and indirect.

A. THE NEW ENGLISH DICTIONARY

Let us imagine that certain words are missing from the English language and that you have been nominated to pass final judgement on the work of a committee which has been trying to invent appropriate words to fill the gaps.

1. The first word on your list is a word to describe *a person who is fat.* (NOUN) Here are the committee's suggestions.

   tine, slipe, chipple, noom, sloame

   You must now throw out three. Of the two you have left which is the fatter sounding?

2. The second word on the list is a word to describe *a person or thing that is thin.* (ADJ) Here are the suggestions.

   glomby, scine, lumbragious, tinch, sloopy

   Reject three. Which of the two you have left is the thinner? Remember that you are concerned with thinness only and no other quality.

3. The third word describes *a party of people walking together in a column for some important and solemn official occasion.* (NOUN) Here are the suggestions.

   tintila, kiggillum, morpumpella, tinkion, drambombion

   Reject three. What are the reasons for your choice between the remaining two?

B. SOUND AND MEANING

Many words are directly imitative. Sound and meaning are obviously related.

1. List six words which represent animal noises.
2. List six words which imitate loud noises.
3. List six words which imitate the sound of moving water.

You may have noticed in your answers to Question 3 that some of the words had a pattern of vowels and consonants in common. Consider the pattern in the words flit, flick, flash, flutter, flee, and flare. You will notice that they all begin with *fl-* and are all concerned with rapid movement.

For each of the following lists of words (a) state the idea the words have in common and (b) identify the common vowel and consonant pattern.

4. slop, slush, sleet, slick, slippery, slimy
5. moan, mourn, doom, gloom, woe, forlorn
6. imp, slit, sip, bit, chink, kitten*

*If, later in your studies, you wish to find out more about sound patterns, we recommend that you read *Sound and Sense* by Laurence Perrine.

C. SOUNDS AT WORK

The sounds of words, then, can be a part of their meaning. Harshness or softness or sibilance is a part of the connotative power of a word. In the following exercises you will consider more closely the part that sound plays in relationship to meaning.

1. Look again at two lines from the poem "Cargoes."

   Dirty British coaster with a salt-caked smoke-stack
   Butting through the Channel in the mad March days.

   If we now substitute synonyms for three words in the original we can write the lines in this way:

   Dirty British coaster with a salt-caked funnel
   Pushing through the Channel in the mad spring days.

   a) What effect does the substitution of 'funnel' for 'smoke-stack' have?
   b) 'pushing' for 'butting'?
   c) 'spring' for 'March'?
   d) Do the substitutions change the feeling of the lines?

2. Consider these lines from a poem by Walter de la Mare.

   And the yeasty surf curdled over the sands,
   The gaunt grey rocks between.

   a) Why, in terms of sound, is 'yeasty' preferable to, say, 'foamy'?
   b) Why 'sands' and not 'sand'?
   c) In the second line there are three hard sounds (*g*aunt *g*rey roc*k*s) on after the other. What is the relationship between the sounds and the things described?
   d) If you were going to draw a picture of this scene, does the line give you any feeling as to the number or shape of the rocks?

3. These lines are from the same poem.

   A snowy, silent, sun-washed drift
   Of sea-birds on the shore.

   a) Which vowel or consonant is most used?

b) What does the repeated use of this sound remind you of?

c) Why would it be counter to de la Mare's purpose to substitute 'quiet' for 'silent' and 'beach' for 'shore'?

4. The following stanza is from the poem "Winter" by Richard Hughes.

> Snow wind-whipt to ice
>   Under a hard sun:
> Stream-runnels curdled hoar
>   Crackle, cannot run.

a) Which letters and groups of letters produce the harsh effect?

b) What sounds contribute to the idea of motion in the first line?

5. The following lines are from a poem by Wilfred Owen called "All Sounds Have Been as Music."

> Gurgle of sluicing surge through hollow rocks,
> The gluttonous lapping of the waves on weeds.

a) In the first line several sounds combine to create the sound of the movement of the water. What are they?

b) Why, in terms of sound, is 'gluttonous' better than 'greedy'?

c) Why, in terms of sound, is 'lapping' a good word to use?

d) The motion of waves is repetitious. Are there any words or repeated consonants which suggest wave after wave?

D. THE SOUND MUST SEEM AN ECHO TO THE SENSE

If a poet strains too hard to make the sounds of the words parallel the meaning, he produces over-obvious sound effects. If the reader suddenly becomes aware of the process, the poet has probably over-written.

1. The following lines are from a poem by Tennyson and they describe Sir Bedivere in full armour carrying the wounded King Arthur on his back. The night is silent and frosty.

   Dry clash'd his harness in the icy caves
   And barren chasms, and all to left and right
   The bare black cliff clang'd round him, as he based
   His feet on juts of slippery crag that rang
   Sharp-smitten with the dint of armed heels—

   a) Which letters and groups of letters does Tennyson work with to produce the sounds made by Sir Bedivere?
   b) Is there a line in the extract where the sound effects become too obvious?

2. This stanza is from Edgar Allen Poe's poem "The Raven." The speaker, sitting alone at night in his room and brooding over his lost love, Lenore, has been disturbed by someone tapping. He goes to the door but nobody is there and he stands peering into the darkness.

   Deep into that darkness peering, long I stood there, wondering, fearing,
   Doubting, dreaming dreams no mortal ever dared to dream before;
   But the silence was unbroken, and the stillness gave no token,
   And the only word there spoken was the whispered word "Lenore!"
   This I whispered, and an echo murmured back the word, "Lenore!"
   Merely this and nothing more.

   a) What are the repeated sounds in the first two lines?
   b) Do they serve any purpose?
   c) What are the dominant sounds in the remaining lines?
   d) Do these sounds successfully parallel meaning or do they become over-obvious?

All the subtle combinations of sounds that poets use have technical names. The most common terms that you will see are *alliteration, assonance,* and *onomatopoeia.* Find out what they mean. But remember that when you are reading a poem you are not looking for an example of alliteration or assonance—you are trying to see how sound is connected with sense. The technical terms merely help you to describe that connection. The eighteenth century poet Alexander Pope in his poem "An Essay on Criticism" wrote:

> The sound must seem an echo to the sense.

This idea should still guide you in your judgements.

Rhythm

RHYTHM PATTERNS

RHYTHM AND MEANING

THE CRAFT OF VERSE

RHYTHM PATTERNS

The words of our language vary in the strength of the sound they produce. Words of more than one syllable usually contain weak and strong sounds. If the relationship of weak and strong syllables in consecutive words follows a pattern, a rhythm develops.

The English language is rich in short, simple words which give it a robust sound. The natural rhythms of our language are also strong. Our nouns, action verbs, adjectives and adverbs usually contain a strong accent. Our connecting words (being verbs, prepositions, articles, etc.) tend to be weakly accented.

A. BASIC PATTERNS (1)

In each of the following sentences put an accent mark over the strong words or syllables. (e.g. The bá·ker sóld a dóz·en doúgh·nuts.)

a) I sat today and read my book.
b) I gave the man a dirty look.
c) To fish we need a line and hook.
d) The dog and cat both bit the cook.

1. How many strong accents are used in each sentence?
2. Compose three sentences which have the same rhythm as these sentences. Maintain the same number of strong beats.
3. Similarly, compose two sentences as above but add one more accent.
4. Similarly, compose two sentences but with one fewer accent.
5. This rhythm is very common in the English language. Why?

When there is a series of words or syllables in which a weak strong, weak-strong accent pattern is developed, the rhythm is imitative of walking or marching. This rhythm is also suitable for underlining simple ideas, simple scenes, or simple movements which we do not wish to over-emphasize.

B. BASIC PATTERNS (2)

Mark the accents in the following sentences.

a) At the back of the bus is a door to go out.

b) On the back of a camel the going is rough.

c) Pouring a drink is a difficult task.

d) Sailing a boat is a wonderful sport.

1. In the first two sentences how many unaccented syllables to each accented syllable are there?
2. What effect does this rhythm have?
3. Which of the two sentences does the rhythm better suit? Why?
4. How does the rhythm in the last two sentences differ from that in the first two sentences? Is the effect similar?
5. Which of the last two sentences does the rhythm better suit? Why?
6. Compose two sentences which follow the same rhythm pattern as (a) and (b).
7. Compose two sentences which follow the same rhythm pattern as (c) and (d).

When there is a series of syllables in which two unaccented syllables precede or follow an accented syllable, the rhythm is similar to a waltz. The rhythm is suitable for emphasizing quick movements such as running, swaying, tumbling.

C. EMPHASIS WITHOUT PATTERN

Indicate the accented words or syllables in the following sentences.

a) From his mouth great shouts of anger poured.

b) Bells rang all day long.

c) Harsh strokes of the lash dug deep wounds.

d) The wind sighed through the willows.

1. What is the chief difference between the way strong accents are used in this exercise and the way they were used in the previous exercises?
2. Explain how the strong accents reinforce the mood and meaning of each sentence.
3. Why would it be difficult to write lines of great length in which each syllable is strongly accented?
4. If it were possible to write lengthy sentences in which each syllable had a strong accent, what effect would be produced?
5. Compose two sentences in which several strong accents follow one another. Attempt to have the accents underline the meaning of the sentence.

When a line contains strong accents which are consecutive, the movement slows down and a sustained feeling or tone results. The repetition of strong accents is very emphatic and adds stress and importance to the words. These strong accents are especially effective in emphasizing emotions and important thoughts.

D. WORKING WITH RHYTHMS

From each of the following pairs, choose the sentence in which the rhythm better emphasizes the thought.

1. I leaped on my horse and galloped away.
   After I leaped on my horse, we galloped off.
2. The Lone Ranger sped into the distance, hot in pursuit of his foe.

   In hot pursuit of his enemy, the Lone Ranger sped into the distance.
3. After much walking, my feet started to ache.
   Walking, walking, walking my feet began to ache.
4. The sound of the thunder increased as it rolled, tumbled, and crashed.

   Rolling and tumbling and crashing, the sound of the thunder increased.

5. Write a short descriptive sentence based on each of the following ideas. Make the rhythm suit the idea described.
   a) soldiers marching
   b) the sound of a siren
   c) a boy falling down stairs
   d) a rabbit running
   e) a man with a limp

RHYTHM AND MEANING

If a poet establishes a definite rhythm pattern, he must be careful not to let that pattern dominate his intentions. If he wishes to impart a serious idea or feeling, his purpose might be ruined if the reader begins mentally bouncing to some obvious rhythm.

A. RHYTHM AS A MASTER

Copy the following nursery rhyme in your exercise book and mark the accented syllables.

> Mary had a little lamb,
> Its fleece was white as snow,
> And everywhere that Mary went
> The lamb was sure to go.
>
> It followed her to school one day:
> That was against the rule;
> It made the children laugh and play
> To see a lamb at school.

1. Describe the basic rhythm pattern of this rhyme.
2. In addition to the scene the rhyme describes, why do children enjoy this rhyme?

The following stanza is from Oliver Goldsmith's amusing description of a minister.

A quiet home had Parson Gray,
  Secluded in a vale;
His daughters all were feminine,
  And all his sons were male.

3. Is the rhythm pattern in this stanza basically the same as that in "Mary Had a Little Lamb"?

4. Why would the poet choose such an obvious rhythm?

The following stanza is from a Scottish ballad. A mother is throwing her daughter over the castle wall to escape the raging fire.

They wrapped her in a pair of sheets,
  And tossed her o'er the wall;
But on the point of Gordon's spear
  She got a deadly fall.

5. Is the rhythm pattern basically the same as in the previous examples in this exercise?

6. Although these ballads often told grim tales, they were very popular and not taken too seriously. Why does the rhythm relieve the grimness of the picture?

The following is the last stanza of a well-known poem of William Wordsworth's. He is sorrowing over the death of a young country beauty.

She lived unknown and few could know
  When Lucy ceased to be;
But she is in her grave, and O,
  The difference to me!

7. Is the rhythm pattern basically the same as that in the previous three examples?

8. Although Wordsworth's intent was very serious in this poem, can you suggest why many modern readers fail to take the poem seriously?

B. RHYTHM AS A SERVANT

Exercise One

The following stanza is from G. K. Chesterton's "The Donkey." The donkey has suffered much abuse from humans because of its ugliness and stubborn will but Chesterton reminds us that the donkey had a moment of greatness when it bore Christ upon its back.

> The tattered outlaw of the earth,
> Of ancient crooked will;
> Starve, scourge, deride me; I am dumb,
> I keep my secret still.

1. Do the first two lines basically follow the "Mary Had a Little Lamb" pattern?
2. In line three, how is the rhythm pattern broken?
3. What purposes does the interruption of the rhythm serve?

Exercise Two

Read the following verse and copy it into your exercise book.

> Run quickly my boys for the gas it is coming!
> Fit on your helmets before it's too late!
> But someone out there was still yelling and stumbling;
> He floundered about like a man at death's gate.

1. Mark the accents. What rhythmic device gives this verse its lilting effect?
2. Does the rhythm pattern suit the thought of the agonizing death which results from breathing in mustard gas?
3. Look at the first line. What would you shout if you were a soldier and saw mustard gas billowing toward you? Would your words have that same sing-songy rhythm?
4. Does the comparison in the last line seem very original?

The following lines are from Wilfred Owen's "Dulce Et Decorum Est." He saw soldiers die from poison gas and he himself was killed while fighting in World War I.

> Gas! GAS! Quick, boys!—An ecstasy of fumbling,
> Fitting the clumsy helmets just in time,
> But someone still was yelling out and stumbling
> And floundering like a man in fire or lime.

5. Is there any obvious rhythm pattern in these four lines?
6. How do the heavy accents on the first four words underline the meaning?
7. Of the remaining seven syllables in the first line, how many are accented? Does the rhythmic feeling underline the meaning?
8. In what way does the rhythmic flow of the second line suit the meaning of the words?
9. Does the rhythm of "and stumbling and floundering" suit the meaning? Why?
10. What would be wrong with the rhythm in relation to meaning if he had finished ". . . like a man in *a* fire or *in* lime"?

Exercise Three

In good poetry rhythm is used subtly. Many good poems have no dominant rhythm pattern. The flow of varying rhythms in support of the meaning is a prime characteristic of a good poem.

The following are the opening lines of Thomas Hardy's "Snow in the Suburbs." Read with a normal tone. Do not attempt to make the lines sing-songy.

> Every branch big with it,
> Bent every twig with it;
> Every fork like a white web-foot;
> Every street and pavement mute:
> Some flakes have lost their way, and grope back upward, when
> Meeting those meandering down they turn and descend again.

1. In the first two lines, what are the accented words? Are they important words?
2. Explain how the rhythm in the first two lines underlines the meaning.
3. How does the rhythm in line three emphasize the picture presented?
4. Why does the rhythm in line four suit the idea?
5. Analyze the last two lines in order to discover how Thomas Hardy uses rhythm very skilfully in his description of gently falling snow.

C. DISCOVERING RHYTHMS

In the following brief quotations rhythms are used subtly. Read the lines in a normal tone. Copy out the quotations and then mark the accented words or syllables. For each quotation explain how the shifting rhythms aid meaning or mood.

1. The farms in the fold of the hill,
        and the clear, carved trees,
    have sunk to the bottom of crystal seas:

LILIAN BOWES LYON

2. Out from the huddled and ugly walls,
    I came sudden, at the city's edge,
    On a blue burst of lake,
    Long lake waves breaking under the sun
    On a spray-flung curve of shore;

CARL SANDBURG

3. The air grew still and seemed to heave,
    And I shot up as the tank exploded,
    And down I came with both legs broken,

EDGAR LEE MASTERS

4. . . . The groaning motor
    Rises in a whine as it grinds in
    The garbage, and between-times
    Groans.

GALWAY KINNELL

THE CRAFT OF VERSE

In the last lesson we saw that rhythm should be a servant to meaning. You are now going to practise some rhythms which, while they may not serve meaning, may offer you an insight into the difficulties of the poet's craft. Many modern poets no longer use the traditional rhythm patterns but it is essential to understand the older patterns before you can fully understand the departures that the modern poets are making.

A. THE BALLAD

One form of the traditional ballad has the following pattern. Read the stanza carefully.

> I sit and scratch my head and think
>   Of words to fit the beat;
> And when I find the proper word,
>   I call it quite a feat.

1. How many lines has the stanza?
2. What is the pattern of accented and non-accented syllables in each line?
3. Which lines have the same number of accented syllables?
4. Which lines end in a rhyme?
5. Using this rhythm and rhyme pattern, write two stanzas which describe one of the following:
   a) getting up in the morning
   b) getting on a crowded bus
   c) the teacher taking attendance in the morning
   d) the approach of a thunder storm

B. THE RHYMING COUPLET

One form of the rhyming couplet has the following pattern. Read the couplets carefully.

> The rhyming couplet takes some skill to write;
> This little one has taken half the night.
> But those who have more skill than I with rhyme
> Could doubtless write the lines in half the time.

1. What is the pattern of accented and non-accented syllables in each line?
2. Is the thought completed in each pair of lines?
3. Using this rhythm and rhyme pattern, write a couplet about one of the following:
   a) being awakened by an alarm clock
   b) having a tooth filled
   c) watching the clock at the end of the last period
   d) eating your favourite food

C. BLANK VERSE

Regular blank verse has the following pattern. Read the lines carefully.

> A lengthy story which a poet writes
> Is often told without the use of rhyme;
> He finds that rhythm patterns are enough.
> The thoughts he wants to tell the reader rest
> On normal accents found in daily speech.

1. What is the pattern of accented and non-accented syllables in the first line?
2. Do the other lines follow the same pattern?
3. Is there any use of rhyme?
4. Is the thought complete in each line?
5. Write six lines of blank verse about one of the following:
   a) waiting for someone who is late
   b) assembling ingredients for a recipe
   c) performing exercises in the gym
   d) a hockey game

D. THE LIMERICK

Limericks are a popular form of entertainment. They are not poems in the real sense of the word, but they are often amusing. Their rhythms and rhymes are obvious. Read the following example carefully.

There was a great lord in Japan,
Whose name on a Tuesday began;
  It carried through Sunday,
  Till twilight on Monday,
And sounded like stones in a can.

By now you should be able to discover the rhythm pattern for yourself. Note the rhyme scheme. Try writing a limerick. Do not worry if your rhythm pattern is not quite the same as the example. The limerick is a form of verse in which the lines can be altered in length without doing much harm; just try to keep a good rhythmic feeling.

RHYTHM: A GENERAL NOTE

You will now have realized that even the writing of simple rhythm patterns is an extremely difficult task. *Remember, however, that rhythm patterns are not important in themselves. They are important only in so far as they reinforce the poem's meaning.*

Figurative Language

SIMILE: POETS ARE LIKE PEOPLE

COMPRESSED COMPARISONS

VERBAL METAPHORS

CONCRETE WORDS

SCENES IN FOCUS

IMAGES

SIMILE: POETS ARE LIKE PEOPLE

In our everyday language we often make comparisons in order to express our thoughts. We might say, "The water is like ice" or "He eats like a horse." Such expressions are very common. We hope to give a clearer idea about one thing by comparing it with another. Unfortunately, these particular expressions are overused. We pay little attention to them because they have grown stale from too much repetition.

These *like* or *as* or *than* comparisons are very common; they are called *similes.* A good writer tends to avoid the similes of everyday language because he knows that the reader will not heed them. A good poet wishes to hold your attention; he will not risk poor similes for fear of losing your interest.

A. DEAD AS A DODO

List eight similes that you have commonly heard. Add your list to those of your classmates. How many different similes are listed? Have you heard all of them before? These are the kind of similes which the poet avoids. They are tired similes.

B. ACCURATE COMPARISONS

Another concern is that the simile be accurate both in logic and in mood. The simile must not accidentally create a false impression. What is inaccurate about the following similes?

1. The enemy helicopter hovered over the wounded men like a hummingbird.
2. The snow drifted down like white paint.
3. The actor's voice was as harsh as an automobile's horn.
4. We could see fish swimming under the ice which was as brittle as china.
5. The fat man waddled along like a barrel.
6. Her sponge cake always turned out as light as feathers.

C. PLUS AND MINUS SIMILES

For each of the following, create two sentences which each contain a simile. The simile in the first sentence should show approval and the simile in the second sentence should show disapproval.

Example: (a) Her face was as delicate as a cameo.
(b) Her face was like a bowl of suet.

1. a policeman
2. a dress
3. a voice
4. a pair of hands
5. a steak

D. CHANTICLEER

The following extract is from a poem by Chaucer which tells the story of a rooster called Chanticleer. Read this extract carefully and then answer the questions that follow.

She had a yard that was enclosed about
By a stockade and a dry ditch without,
In which she kept a cock called Chanticleer.
In all the land for crowing he'd no peer;
His voice was jollier than the organ blowing
In church on Sundays, he was great at crowing.
His comb was redder than fine coral, tall
And battlemented like a castle wall,
His bill was black and shone as bright as jet,
Like azure were his legs and they were set
On azure toes with nails of lily white,
Like burnished gold his feathers, flaming bright.

Word meanings: *peer*—equal
jet—a brilliant black semi-precious stone
azure—sky blue
burnished—polished

Questions

1. List the similes the poet uses.

2. Explain in what way Chanticleer's comb was like a battlemented wall.
3. Four of the similes describe Chanticleer's colour. Do they have anything else in common? Would it make much difference to our picture of Chanticleer if Chaucer had written *His comb was redder than a drunkard's nose,* and *His bill was black and shone like boot-polish*?
4. Two of the similes tell us indirectly how large and powerful the rooster was. Which are those similes? How do they suggest Chanticleer's power?
5. Chaucer has a purpose in this extract which goes beyond simple description. He is telling us, through his choice of simile, something about Chanticleer's character. Briefly describe Chanticleer's character.

E. WORKING WITH SIMILES

For further practice, choose one of the following ideas and write a paragraph of five or six sentences. Make sure that the paragraph contains several similes and that they all serve the mood or idea you wish to create.

1. the slow, swaying descent of a parachute jumper on a bright summer's day.
2. the rapid advance of a violent thunderstorm.
3. a particularly self-confident young man calling for his girlfriend.
4. A family gorging itself with food on Thanksgiving Day.

F. MAKING JUDGEMENTS

The following quotations contain similes which range in quality from the good to the startlingly bad. Read them carefully and then in each case (a) state whether you think the simile good or bad and (b) give reasons for your decision.

1. Ghost-like I paced round the haunts of my childhood.

CHARLES LAMB

2. They're tearing down, tearing up
this city, block by block.
Rooms, cut in half,
hang like flayed carcasses,

ADRIENNE RICH

3. Her neck is like a stately tower.

THOMAS LODGE

4. Her lips are like two budded roses.

THOMAS LODGE

5. And—with my cheek on one of those green stones
That, fleeced with moss, under the shady trees,
Lay round me, scattered like a flock of sheep—

WILLIAM WORDSWORTH

6. ...... the youthful hue
Sits on thy skin like morning dew.

ANDREW MARVELL

7. The Worldly Hope men set their Hearts upon
Turns Ashes, or it prospers; and anon,
    Like Snow upon the Desert's dusty Face
Lighting a little hour or two, is gone.

EDWARD FITZGERALD

An understanding of the simile is a useful introduction to the study of more subtle uses of comparative language. The modern poet uses simile sparingly. Most poets nowadays tend to express themselves in the more compressed forms of comparison which are discussed in the following lessons.

COMPRESSED COMPARISONS

A. In the previous lesson each comparison contained the word *like*, *as*, or *than*. These are indicators. *Like*, *as*, and *than* indicate that a comparison is being made.

What happens if we leave out the indicator words when making a comparison? Consider the two short sentences which follow:

a) His muscles are *like* iron.
b) His muscles are iron.

Answer the following:

1. Has the meaning changed in the second sentence?
2. Which sentence is further removed from actual truth? Why?
3. Which sentence requires more imagination to understand?
4. Which sentence would make the stronger impression on the reader? Why?
5. State two qualities which 'iron' could have in common with 'muscles.'
6. In summary, state three reasons why a writer might wish to write the second sentence rather than the first.

Most comparisons which leave out the words *like*, *as*, or *than* are called *metaphors.*

B. BUILDING METAPHORS

Just as *His muscles are iron* is less obvious and demands more imagination than *His muscles are like iron*, it is possible to be less obvious still. Does the phrase *his iron muscles* have the same meaning as the sentence *His muscles are (like) iron?* Obviously the same meaning is understood, but fewer words have been used and more imagination is required to recognize that a comparison has been made.

Rewrite the following sentences leaving out the word *like.* Second, shorten the idea to a single phrase and then create a sentence using your imagination.

Example: The air was like ice.
The air was icy.
The icy air blew from the north and chilled me to the bone.

(It may be necessary to alter the word to its adjectival or participial form.)

1. The boxer's ear is like a cauliflower.
2. Her skin was like satin.

3. The sea was like turquoise.
4. His nerves were like steel.
5. His temper was like fire.

C. EXPANDING METAPHORS

In the previous exercise the comparisons were narrowed down to a phrase. Of the two things compared, one was stated by the noun and the other by the adjective. Very similar metaphors sometimes occur when a noun is modified by a prepositional phrase. For example the sentence:

The edge of the canyon projects like a lip

can be reduced in the following way:

The edge of the canyon is like a lip.
The edge of the canyon is a lip.
The lip of the canyon.

In the following exercise expand the metaphor into a fully explanatory sentence.

Example: *The buzz of the saw* may be expanded to *The noise made by the saw is like the buzzing made by bees.*

1. the march of time
2. the canopy of the sky
3. the muttering of the stream
4. the grumbling of the thunder
5. the barking of the guns

D. WORKING WITH METAPHORS

1. The following are the first three lines of Alfred Noyes' "The Highwayman."

The wind was a torrent of darkness among the gusty trees,
The moon was a ghostly galleon tossed upon cloudy seas,
The road was a ribbon of moonlight over the purple moor.

a) What two things are compared in the first line?
b) State what common characteristics they possess.

c) Line two employs three metaphors. State what they are.

d) What two things are compared in the third line?

e) What kind of night is being described?

f) Is the poem going to be peaceful or full of action?

g) Are pleasant or unpleasant things going to happen? Why?

2. The following lines are from Thomas Gray's "Ode on the Death of a Favourite Cat." The cat is staring with fascination into a tub containing goldfish.

> The fair round face, the snowy beard,
> The velvet of her paws;
> Her coat that with the tortoise vies,*
> Her ears of jet, and emerald eyes,
> She saw; and purr'd applause.

a) Does the word 'snowy' imply anything more than that the cat's face is white?

b) State three characteristics that velvet has.

c) State two things which tortoise shell could have in common with the fur of a cat.

d) What is jet?

e) What is an emerald?

f) How many things to which the cat is compared have considerable value in our world?

g) Briefly state what the author meant to convey by the description of the cat.

3. The following are brief quotations from various poems. State the two things being compared. Explain why the comparisons are apt. A few of the quotations may contain more than one comparison.

a) The boat put in at dead of night.

b) The stars are in bloom.

**vies*—competes.

c) Hold fast to dreams
For when dreams go
Life is a barren field
Frozen with snow.

d) No man is an island.

e) And the hoarse whisper of the corn.

f) I wield the flail of the lashing hail.

g) . . . . . and the bleak winds moan
About the naked uplands.

h) . . . . . Down in the west
The brimming plains beneath the sunset rest,
One burning sea of gold.

VERBAL METAPHORS

In the previous lesson we have seen that metaphors are sometimes created by the use of adjectives, participles, or prepositional phrases. It takes imagination for the writer to create such metaphors and it takes imagination for the reader to grasp them. When used well the metaphor adds power and vividness to the author's ideas.

A. Consider the two sentences which follow:

(a) The strong winds did considerable damage to the trees.

(b) The wind howled and shrieked through the woods, clawing and grabbing at branches until it stripped limbs from trunks and uprooted entire trees and tossed them lifeless to the ground.

Answer the following:

1. Which sentence gives the better idea of the strength of the wind?
2. Which sentence would you use if you wished to convince someone that there has been a bad storm? Why?

3. Does the wind have hands or paws for grabbing or nails for clawing? Does the wind have vocal chords so that it is able to shriek and howl?
4. What things, real or imaginery, could have the power to howl, shriek, claw, grab, strip, uproot?
5. Does the wind actually possess all this ability or has a comparison been made?
6. What part of speech was used to show the extent of the power of the wind?
7. Why is this part of speech powerful?

From the analysis of the second sentence, it is obvious that a comparison can be made even though one of the two things being compared is not stated; the metaphor is completed by our imagination. One thing is *stated*, the other is *implied*. In such *implied metaphors*, the verb is the key.

B. EXPANDING VERBAL METAPHOR

The following sentences contain implied verbal metaphors. Complete the comparison which the sentence implies. Remember that the *verb* is the key.

Examples: (a) The orders shot from the sergeant's mouth. (implied)
The orders shot like bullets from the sergeant's mouth. (stated)
(b) The lawyer sifted the evidence.
The lawyer sifted the evidence like a farmer sifting wheat.

1. As I burrowed deeper into the problem I became more confused.
2. The waves lapped at the shore.
3. The runner stole second base.
4. Suddenly, the ravine yawned at my feet.
5. The gossips buzzed the scandal through the town.
6. Ideas flew through my head.

C. WORKING WITH VERBAL METAPHOR

The implied metaphor is capable of conveying an idea or feeling with great intensity. It grasps the imagination and, because an action verb is used, it conveys a sense of motion to the picture it creates. Rewrite the following generalized sentences in a more forceful way by using implied metaphor.

Examples: (a) *The breeze felt very pleasant*, a vague generalization, could become *The breeze stroked my hair and caressed my cheeks.* The breeze has been compared to a lover.

(b) *The sun was terribly hot* could become *The sun burned into my neck, searing and scorching so that my skin blistered.* The heat of the sun has been compared to fire to indicate the degree of its strength.

1. The various guns made a lot of noise.
2. The half-back displayed tremendous speed as he eluded the defence and ran for a touchdown.
3. I was very happy.
4. The snow was gently drifting down the street.
5. She was very graceful.
6. The lights of the city were pretty.
7. The armoured corps moved swiftly.
8. In the north, night comes slowly.

D. METAPHOR IN CONTEXT (1)

The following are the opening lines of Karl Shapiro's "Auto Wreck." He is describing an ambulance going to the scene of an accident.

Its quick soft silver bell beating, beating,
And down the dark one ruby flare
Pulsing out red light like an artery,
The ambulance at top speed floating down
Past beacons and illuminated clocks
Wings in a heavy curve, dips down,
And brakes speed, entering the crowd.

1. In the first line 'beating, beating' suggests a comparison with what? Remember that the ambulance is going to the scene of an accident.
2. In line two the adjective 'ruby' is used to describe the signal light. What color is a ruby? Is it valuable? At an accident what else might be seen that is the color of a ruby? Is it also valuable?
3. Lines two and three contain an obvious simile. What two things have been compared? Why did the poet use the word 'pulsing'?
4. By the use of several metaphoric ideas, the poet has reminded us of what necessary life functions?
5. What do you imagine the scene will be like when the ambulance arrives at its destination? Why?
6. In the remaining four lines identify the verbs.
7. The speed and movements of the ambulance are being compared to what?
8. Does the emphasis on speed suggest anything to you?
9. How do the last four lines reinforce the idea contained in the opening three lines?

E. METAPHOR IN CONTEXT (2)

Read the following poem carefully.

SOLITAIRE

When night drifts along the streets of the city,
And sifts down between the uneven roofs,
My mind begins to poke and peer.
It plays at ball in odd, blue Chinese gardens,
And shakes wrought dice-cups in Pagan Temples
Amid the broken flutings of white pillars.
It dances with purple and yellow crocuses in its hair,
And its feet shine as they flutter over the drenched grasses.
How light and laughing my mind is,
When all good folk have put out their bedroom candles,
And the city is still!

AMY LOWELL

1. With what has the approach of night been compared?
2. What mood is created by the first two lines?
3. Does the mind have the ability to 'poke and peer'? What is the metaphor here?
4. Who usually plays ball?
5. What is a person who likes to play with dice usually called?
6. What other unexpected abilities does the poet's mind possess?
7. Why did these activities take place in Chinese gardens and Pagan Temples?
8. How does the mood created by these activities contrast with the mood of the opening lines?
9. What normal ability that we all possess is being illustrated by the series of metaphors in this poem?
10. Why does the poet's mind only show this ability after everyone else is asleep and the noises created by the daytime activity have been deadened? Do you think she may be criticizing the way we spend our waking hours? Why?
11. Consider the last two lines in contrast to the preceding lines. Do you think the poet feels herself to be one of the 'good folk'? Why?

CONCRETE WORDS

Beware of judging a poem by the number of similes or metaphors it contains. Many poets have used *stated* similes and metaphor very sparingly if at all. *Implied* metaphor, because it is more subtle, is used somewhat more. But most of the power in vast numbers of poems stems from the concrete detail they contain. This fact is especially true of modern poetry.

A. A WORD IS WORTH A THOUSAND PICTURES

A Chinese poet, Tu Fu, wrote this remarkable poem some twelve hundred years ago. It is remarkable for its content as well as for its length.

Blue is the smoke of war, white the bones of men.

There are no metaphors in the poem. No conclusion or meaning is stated in the poem.

1. Write a paragraph of five or six sentences based on what the words 'Blue is the smoke of war' suggest to your imagination.
2. Similarly, write a paragraph based on what 'white the bones of men' suggests to your imagination.
3. Consider your two paragraphs. What can you conclude about war?
4. What idea was Tu Fu expressing in his poem?

Tu Fu realized the power of a few concrete words to suggest a great series of mental pictures. We do not even have to have witnessed war to envision the destruction and slaughter. By filling in with our imaginations more detail than is stated, we are forced to draw certain conclusions. With six concrete words, Tu Fu expressed his feelings about war.

B. Consider another Chinese poem. This one is by Lu Yu and was written about eight hundred years ago.

DEATH

Old Chang died after three years' sickness;
Old Wu suddenly went out one night.
My body is hard like steel.
I lean on the door, gazing at the green hill.

1. Old Chang and Old Wu have died. Their deaths were different. Suggest the causes of their deaths.
2. The third line contains a simile. What is the poet's physical condition? How old is the poet?

3. What does 'green hill' suggest to your imagination?
4. What thoughts are in the poet's mind as he gazes at the hill?
5. What ideas concerning human existence has the poet suggested in these four lines?

C. This is part of an old Scottish ballad in which the language has been modernized. Two corbies (a kind of crow which eats dead flesh) are overheard talking. They present this concrete picture.

THE TWO CORBIES

In behind that old sod dike,
I know there lies a new-slain knight;
And nobody knows that he lies there,
But his hawk, his hound, and lady fair.

His hound is to the hunting gone,
His hawk to fetch the wild-fowl home,
His lady took another mate,
So we may make our dinner sweet.

You sit on his fine white neck,
And I'll pick out his pretty blue eye,
With a lock of his golden hair
We'll line our nest when it grows bare.

1. What are the two important facts stated in the first stanza?
2. Select any one of the first three lines in the second stanza and briefly describe the scene that comes to your imagination. Is the mood pleasant? If you had chosen one of the remaining two lines would the mood be the same?
3. Most of the words in the third stanza would ordinarily have pleasant connotations. What particular word changes the mood to one of horror?

4. Briefly describe the mental picture created by the second line of this stanza.
5. Who do you think killed the knight? Why was he killed?
6. Our imaginations have created two contrasting scenes from the concrete detail in stanzas two and three. What is the effect of this contrast?
7. What view of human love and friendship has been illustrated?
8. How does the concrete detail of the last stanza underline the grimness of what has happened?
9. Does the rhythm pattern of the poem make the mood more or less grim?
10. To what extent has the poet used similes or metaphors to create his emotional effect?

D. Read the following poem carefully.

THE SONG OF THE OLD MOTHER

I rise in the dawn, and I kneel and blow
Till the seed of the fire flicker and glow;
And then I must scrub and bake and sweep
Till stars are beginning to blink and peep;
And the young lie long and dream in their bed
Of the matching of ribbon for bosom and head,
And their day goes over in idleness,
And they sigh if the wind but lift a tress:
While I must work because I am old,
And the seed of the fire gets feeble and cold.

WILLIAM BUTLER YEATS

Consider the first four lines.

1. What four tasks are we told she performs?
2. What other tasks do you think she might perform?
3. Does she work alone?

4. How long each day does she work?
5. Describe the old woman as you imagine her.

Consider the next six lines.

6. What do the young people do while the mother starts the fire?
7. What do the young people do during the rest of the day?
8. What does the mention of 'ribbons' and 'tress' suggest about the interests of the young?

Consider the last two lines.

9. Explain why the woman works so hard.
10. How does the picture in the last line contrast with the picture in the second line of the poem?
11. Does the metaphor 'the seed of the fire' refer only to the fire on the hearth?

Yeats used metaphor sparingly to underline an idea which he had already stated in a series of concrete word pictures. The metaphors used in this poem flow easily out of a much larger bulk of vivid detail.

SCENES IN FOCUS

We saw in the last lesson that our minds seize upon vivid, concrete words and enlarge upon them. Such words form pictures in our minds. Good poets, just like good photographers, always try to create clear, sharp pictures. If a poet uses a word inaccurately or vaguely, the picture becomes weak and blurred. His observation, and the words and phrases he uses to describe what he has observed, must be vivid and well-focused. Vague and unfocused language has little connotative power. It is the *concrete* word, the sharp detail, which makes us feel strongly.

A. Read the following poem carefully.

LEISURE

What is this life if, full of care,
We have no time to stand and stare.

No time to stand beneath the boughs
And stare as long as sheep or cows.

No time to see, when woods we pass,
Where squirrels hide their nuts in grass.

No time to see, in broad daylight,
Streams full of stars, like stars at night.

No time to turn at Beauty's glance,
And watch her feet, how they can dance.

No time to wait till her mouth can
Enrich that smile her eyes began.

A poor life this if, full of care,
We have no time to stand and stare.

W. H. DAVIES

The poet is comparing the rush and bustle of our lives with the beauties of the natural world which we are too busy to see.

1. Make a list of all the details he describes which he thinks should make us 'stand and stare.'
2. With what, in verses 5 and 6, is the poet comparing natural beauties?

The following verses are from a *parody* of W. H. Davies' poetry. (A *parody* is an imitation of an author's way of writing designed to make fun of the writing and show its weaknesses.)

MR. W. H. DAVIES

I'm sure that you would never guess
    The tales I hear from birds and flowers,
Without them sure 'twould be a mess
    I'd make of all the summer hours;
But these fair things they make for me
A lovely life of joy and glee.

I saw some sheep upon some grass,
    The sheep were fat, the grass was green,
The sheep were white as clouds that pass,
    And greener grass was never seen;
I thought, "Oh, how my bliss is deep,
With such green grass and such fat sheep!"

J. C. SQUIRE

1. In the second verse Squire writes '*some* sheep' and '*some* grass.' He tells us that the sheep are 'fat' and the grass is 'green.' How much have you learned about the scene?

2. In the third line of verse two he describes the sheep as 'white as clouds.' Is this an original simile?

3. Look at the word 'bliss' in the fifth line of the second verse. How deep an emotion is *bliss*? Would 'green grass' and 'fat sheep' cause you to feel blissful?

4. Reread the whole of the second verse. Why is it funny? Do you think the 'I' in the poem is meant to be an intelligent person?

5. In "Leisure" Davies wished us to feel that the beauties of the natural world were more important than the meaningless rush of our daily lives. There is nothing silly in such an idea. Yet he fails to convince us because he fails to make us see or feel that beauty.

   a) Are his details vivid? Choose one detail and examine it closely.

   b) Can you see or feel 'Beauty'? Is Beauty a concrete thing?

   c) In what way are streams and squirrels like a beautiful woman dancing?

   d) What did he mean by 'streams full of stars'? If the stream was not literally 'full' of stars, perhaps he is talking of sunlight glinting on the water. Is glinting sunlight particularly like stars in the night sky? What are the differences? Is this a successful metaphor?

e) When he writes 'like stars at night,' are the last two words necessary? Are the four words necessary? Have you heard of 'broad daylight' before? Is it an original expression? Read both lines of this verse again carefully.

6. Perhaps you can see more clearly now why Sir John Squire thought that 'some sheep upon some grass' was typical of Davies' vague and unfocused work. Here is one last example of slack writing.

   a) If you were standing under a bough staring in the same way that sheep and cows stare, what expression might you have on your face?

   b) What connotations do you think Davies intended the second verse to have?

B. Read the following poem carefully.

NEW SNOW

The pines are white-powdered,
    Delicately tossed
With fairy filigrees
    Of silver frost.

The top of the mountain
    Is lost in a cloud,
While the world is silent
    And the winds unloud.

Drink in the beauty,
    The shadows .... the glow ....
The wonder of winter
    And new white snow!

C. B. ROWLES

1. Which words in the first verse have pleasing connotations?

2. What is the meaning of 'filigrees'?

3. What are 'fairy filigrees'?

4. Do fairies cover pine trees with frost?

5. Do connotations remain pleasing when they are inaccurate or illogical?

6. How loud is an 'unloud' wind? Why did the poet use this word which is not to be found in a dictionary? Is the reason a good reason?

7. Does the writer use concrete language? (Illustrate your answer by examining words in the poem. Pay particular attention to the third stanza.)

The following verse is from the poem called "Snow in the Suburbs."

Every branch big with it,
Bent every twig with it;
Every fork like a white web-foot;
Every street and pavement mute:
Some flakes have lost their way, and grope back upward, when
Meeting those meandering down they turn and descend again.
The palings are glued together like a wall,
And there is no waft of wind with the fleecy fall.

THOMAS HARDY

Comparisons

Compare the following details from "New Snow" and "Snow in the Suburbs."

1. 'the world is silent' and 'Every street and pavement mute.'

2. 'the winds unloud' and 'no waft of wind.'

3. Hardy wrote 'like a white web-foot.' Why did he use the word 'white'? Is C. B. Rowles telling you anything when she writes 'white snow'?

4. Can you find any uses of rhythm to reinforce meaning in either poem?

5. Select from one of the poems two or three details which you think are carefully observed and well-expressed.
6. Which poem is the more concrete, the more real?

In Conclusion

Write a brief essay explaining what you have learned about poetry from your reading of "Leisure" by W. H. Davies and "New Snow" by C. B. Rowles. Illustrate your ideas by quoting from the poems.

IMAGES

The exercises you have completed have introduced the basic skills required in reading poetry. Some poems, however, defy analysis; they demand instead a sensitive act of recognition. The harder the student tries to apply to them the reasonable and logical skills he has been learning the more baffled he will become.

Read the following poem and then try to think about it analytically.

THE BARLEY FIELD

Up the barley rows
stitching, stitching them together,
a butterfly goes.

SORA (1648-1710)

The poem is simply an exclamation of pleasure at the sight of the butterfly and the recognition that its flight is like the diagonal movements of a needle stitching. We can admire the way the poet catches the movement by repetition and we can feel the clever way the last line "releases" the poem as if the poet was exclaiming in delight but the meaning of the poem remains in the delighted recognition itself. We cannot analyse; we can only respond.

Many poets write brief and delicate verses purely to capture a stray feeling or a sight which pleases them. If we recognize their picture or share the way they feel we can exclaim with them, "Yes! How beautiful!" or "That's exactly the way it is!" If you find poems of this type in the anthology which do not strike a chord in you, do not worry over them. Somewhere there will be a poem which has created "your" picture or feeling and which can move you to a response.

William Carlos Williams has been widely criticized for the following poem. He has also been widely praised.

THE RED WHEELBARROW

so much depends
upon

a red wheel
barrow

glazed with rain
water

beside the white
chickens.

Many people have said, "What does it *mean*?" And those who like it reply, "What a silly question!" We might ask what Williams meant by the lines

"so much depends
upon . . . ."

but a simple answer might be that much depends *for him*.

If a common, everyday sight seems beautiful or inexplicably significant to you, you will perhaps be able to share Williams' poem. All he is saying is that this particular sight is, for him, important and moving. If this poem means nothing to you then the search for "your" poem must continue.

PART TWO

Armadale Avenue Revisited

Street of my boyhood
(I lived right around the corner),
quiet, leaf-heavy street
of West Toronto.

Here,
behind that house, in the lane,
from garage roofs we ambushed
the Nelles Street gang,
pinned them down with catapults,
then, out of acorns,
forgot all our strategy
and ran like hell.

Out this door
on Christmas Day
of all days, that queer girl
came sleep-walking, nightgown and all,
and even the snow underfoot
couldn't waken her.

At this number lived
the grease-monkey boys,
(their Stutz Touring shined
to a blinding dazzle),
who sometimes took me
as heart-pounding passenger
out the Queen Elizabeth,
to run her, gun her
past eighty on a straight stretch,
with the extra spice
of maybe a speed-cop
coming out of nowhere.

On this lawn
I pounded and bloodied
my next-to-worst enemy,
and curiously found
it wasn't fun any more. . .

But tonight it's only
ghosts I see around these houses,
the old gang gone,
every one of them;
some killed in war,
some from natural causes,
the rest, I can guess,
growing fat and middle-aged
like me.

But not one of them
comes back here, I know,
they've got better sense:

just the crazy poet
well-hooked on the past,
a sucker for memories.

RAYMOND SOUSTER

Snow in the Suburbs

Every branch big with it,
Bent every twig with it;
Every fork like a white web-foot;
Every street and pavement mute:
Some flakes have lost their way, and grope back upward, when
Meeting those meandering down they turn and descend again.
The palings are glued together like a wall,
And there is no waft of wind with the fleecy fall.

A sparrow enters the tree,
Whereon immediately
A snow-lump thrice his own slight size
Descends on him and showers his head and eyes,
And overturns him,
And near inurns him,
And lights on a nether twig, when its brush
Starts off a volley of other lodging lumps with a rush.

The steps are a blanched slope,
Up which, with feeble hope,
A black cat comes, wide-eyed and thin;
And we take him in.

THOMAS HARDY

City Trees

The trees along this city street,
Save for the traffic and the trains,
Would make a sound as thin and sweet
As trees in country lanes.

And people standing in their shade
Out of a shower, undoubtedly
Would hear such music as is made
Upon a country tree.

Oh, little leaves that are so dumb
Against the shrieking city air,
I watch you when the wind has come,—
I know what sound is there.

EDNA ST. VINCENT MILLAY

The Harbor

Passing through huddled and ugly walls,
By doorways where women haggard
Looked from their hunger-deep eyes,
Haunted with shadows of hunger-hands,
Out from the huddled and ugly walls,
I came sudden, at the city's edge,
On a blue burst of lake,
Long lake waves breaking under the sun
On a spray-flung curve of shore;
And a fluttering storm of gulls,
Masses of great gray wings
And flying white bellies
Veering and wheeling free in the open.

CARL SANDBURG

Hot Cake

Winter has come; fierce is the cold;
In the sharp morning air new-risen we meet.
Rheum freezes in the nose;
Frost hangs about the chin.
For hollow bellies, for chattering teeth and shivering knees
What better than hot cake?
Soft as the down of spring,
Whiter than autumn floss!
Dense and swift the steam
Rises, swells and spreads.
Fragrance flies through the air,
Is scattered far and wide,
Steals down along the wind and wets
The covetous mouth of passer-by.
Servants and grooms
Cast sidelong glances, munch the empty air.
They lick their lips who serve;
While lines of envious lackeys by the wall
Stand dryly swallowing.

SHU HUI (A.D. 265-306)
Translated by Arthur Waley

Things Made by Iron

Things made by iron and handled by steel
are born dead, they are shrouds, they soak life out of us.
Till after a long time, when they are old and have steeped
in our life
they begin to be soothed and soothing: then we throw
them away.

D. H. LAWRENCE

Things Men Have Made

Things men have made with wakened hands, and put
soft life into
are awake through years with transferred touch, and go
on glowing
for long years.
And for this reason, some old things are lovely
warm still with the life of forgotten men who made
them.

D. H. LAWRENCE

The Transformation

We called them Chinks:
late April to November
they worked the flats south of the Humber bridge
sun-up to sunset, pushing lettuce, carrots
and cabbage out of the black earth.
Lived in broken-down,
unpainted farmhouses, and no one ever
saw a woman in any doorway,
though they must have been there.

We stole their carrots,
and when they caught us chased us laughingly
with their curved knives, giving up
when they saw us running out of breath.
Then one day
the real-estate boys got busy,
and in a month our Chinese were gone,
the neat straight-as-arrow rows
ploughed under by bulldozers, farmhouses ripped apart for
firewood.

Today you can walk
through the clapboard subdivision
thrown up on the spot, and you won't smell one rotten cabbage,
won't see one row of carrots, won't spot one flight of crows
start suddenly downwind.
Even the old bridge is gone,
the river beside it tamed and freshly channelled;
and certainly
no Chinamen
with curved knives to chase today's children....

RAYMOND SOUSTER

Prelude

The winter evening settles down
With smells of steaks in passageways.
Six o'clock.
The burnt-out ends of smoky days.
And now a gusty shower wraps
The grimy scraps
Of withered leaves about your feet
And newspapers from vacant lots;
The showers beat
On broken blinds and chimney-pots,
And at the corner of the street
A lonely cab-horse steams and stamps.
And then the lighting of the lamps.

T. S. ELIOT

Saturday Night

Every five minutes they turn,
with their tires like sirens,
tusking the dirt up on the creek road,
and drive back through town—

slowing down on Main Street, manoeuvring
between the farmers' cars, hooting
at girls on the pavement who reply
with little hen movements, laughing, waiting.

The boys sport leather jackets and levis,
but that's their underwear,
the car is their real clothing:
at Taylor's Corner they turn again,
their Hollywood mufflers
making sounds furious, derisive, vulgar—
like a bear growling and breaking wind,

and roar through Main Street again.

ALDEN NOWLAN

Klaxon

All day cars mooed and shrieked,
Hollered and bellowed and wept
Upon the road.
They slid by with bits of fur attached,
Fox-tails and rabbit-legs,
The skulls and horns of deer,
Cars with yellow spectacles
Or motorcycle monocle,
Cars whose gold eyes burnt
With a too-rich battery,
Murderous cars and manslaughter cars,
Ownerless, passengerless, driverless,
They came to anyone
And with headlights full of tears
Begged for a master,
For someone to drive them,
For the familiar chauffeur.
Limousines covered with pink slime
Of children's blood
Turned into the open fields
And fell over into ditches,
The wheels kicking helplessly.
Taxis begged trees to step inside,
Automobiles begged of posts
The whereabouts of their mother.
But no one wished to own them any more,
Everyone wished to walk.

JAMES REANEY

We Are Going to See the Rabbit

We are going to see the rabbit,
We are going to see the rabbit.
Which rabbit, people say?
Which rabbit, ask the children?
Which rabbit?
The only rabbit,
The only rabbit in England,
Sitting behind a barbed-wire fence
Under the floodlights, neon lights,
Sodium lights,
Nibbling grass
On the only patch of grass
In England, in England
(Except the grass by the hoarding
Which doesn't count.)
We are going to see the rabbit
And we must be there on time.

First we shall go by escalator,
Then we shall go by underground,
And then we shall go by motorway
And then by helicopterway,
And the last ten yards we shall have to go
On foot.

And now we are going
All the way to see the rabbit,
We are nearly there,
We are longing to see it,
And so is the crowd
Which is here in thousands
With mounted policemen
And big loudspeakers
And bands and banners,
And everyone has come a long way.

But soon we shall see it
Sitting and nibbling
The blades of grass
On the only patch of grass
In—but something has gone wrong!
Why is everyone so angry,
Why is everyone jostling
And slanging and complaining?

The rabbit has gone,
Yes, the rabbit has gone.
He has actually burrowed down into the earth
And made himself a warren, under the earth,
Despite all these people.
And what shall we do?
What *can* we do?

It is all a pity, you must be disappointed,
Go home and do something else for today,
Go home again, go home for today.
For you cannot hear the rabbit, under the earth,
Remarking rather sadly to himself, by himself,
As he rests in his warren, under the earth:
'It won't be long, they are bound to come,
They are bound to come and find me, even here.'

ALAN BROWNJOHN

Chanson Innocent

in Just-
spring   when the world is mud-
luscious the little
lame balloonman

whistles   far   and wee

and eddieandbill come
running from marbles and
piracies and it's
spring

when the world is puddle-wonderful

the queer
old balloonman whistles
far   and   wee
and bettyandisabel come dancing

from hop-scotch and jump-rope and

it's
spring
and

          the

                    goat-footed

balloonMan   whistles
far
and
wee

e. e. cummings

from

Like This Together

They're tearing down, tearing up
this city, block by block.
Rooms, cut in half,
hang like flayed carcasses,
their old roses in rags,
famous streets have forgotten
where they were going. Only
a fact could be so dreamlike.
They're tearing down the houses
we met and lived in,
soon our two bodies will be all
left standing from that era.

ADRIENNE RICH

Factory Windows

Factory windows are always broken.
    Somebody's always throwing bricks,
Somebody's always heaving cinders,
    Playing ugly Yahoo tricks.

Factory windows are always broken.
    Other windows are let alone.
No one throws through chapel-window
    The bitter, snarling derisive stone.

Factory windows are always broken.
    Something or other is going wrong.
Something is rotten—I think, in Denmark.
    End of the factory-window song.

VACHEL LINDSAY

Ghostly Story

In winter twilight on a side street,
black—touched at the edges by snow,
with secondhand cars parked headlight to trunk,
a deadeye glow in each window,
I heard a 'clip-clop,' 'clip-clop'
ringing as if the earth was hollow.

And all white with his tall ears
dusting the underside of heaven, a Clydesdale
with mighty brushes of hair on his hooves
swelled and swept from the shadows
. . . One moment I stood in his friendly eye
then like a lord he passed me.

With all the pride of his vanished race
he switched his big wind of a tail,
then turned a corner
and his hoofbeats abruptly stilled,
leaving one steaming brown bun
and a hush as if sparrows were listening.

MILTON ACORN

The Garbage Truck

The garbage disposal truck
Like a huge hunched animal
That sucks in garbage in the place
Where other animals evacuate it
Whines, as the cylinder in the rear
Threshes up the trash and garbage,
Where two men in rubber suits
(It must be raining outside)
Heap it in. The groaning motor
Rises in a whine as it grinds in
The garbage, and between-times
Groans. It whines and groans again.
All about it as it moves down
5th Street is the clatter of trashcans,
The crashes of them as the sanitary engineers
Bounce them on the sidewalk.
If it is raining outside
You can only tell by looking
In puddles, under the lifted streetlamps.

It would be the spring rain.

GALWAY KINNELL

The Miller

The Miller was a chap of sixteen stone,
A great stout fellow big in brawn and bone.
He did well out of them, for he could go
And win the ram at any wrestling show.
Broad, knotty and short-shouldered, he would boast
He could heave any door off hinge and post,
Or take a run and break it with his head.
His beard, like any sow or fox, was red
And broad as well, as though it were a spade;
And, at its very tip, his nose displayed
A wart on which there stood a tuft of hair
Red as the bristles in an old sow's ear.
His nostrils were as black as they were wide,
He had a sword and buckler at his side,
His mighty mouth was like a furnace door.
A wrangler and buffoon, he had a store
Of tavern stories, filthy in the main.
His was a master-hand at stealing grain.
He felt it with his thumb and thus he knew
Its quality and took three times his due—
A thumb of gold, by God, to gauge an oat!
He wore a hood of blue and a white coat.
He liked to play his bagpipes up and down
And that was how he brought us out of town.

CHAUCER
Translated by Nevil Coghill

Alison

And she had plucked her eyebrows into bows,
Slenderly arched they were, and black as sloes.
And a more truly blissful sight to see
She was than blossom on a cherry-tree,
And softer than the wool upon a wether.
And by her girdle hung a purse of leather,
Tasselled in silk, with metal droplets, pearled.
If you went seeking up and down the world
The wisest man you met would have to wrench
His fancy to imagine such a wench.
She had a shining colour, gaily tinted,
And brighter than a florin newly minted,
And when she sang it was as loud and quick
As any swallow perched above a rick.
And she would skip or play some game or other
Like any kid or calf behind its mother.
Her mouth was sweet as mead or honey—say
A hoard of apples lying in the hay.
Skittish she was and jolly as a colt,
Tall as a mast and upright as a bolt
Out of a bow. Her collaret revealed
A brooch as big as boss upon a shield.
High shoes she wore, and laced them to the top.
She was a daisy, O a lollypop.

CHAUCER
Translated by Nevil Coghill

Roger the Cook

They had a Cook with them who stood alone
For boiling chicken with a marrow-bone,
Sharp flavouring-powder and a spice for savour,
He could distinguish London ale by flavour,
And he could roast and seethe and broil and fry,
Make good thick soup and bake a tasty pie.
But a great pity, as it seemed to me,
Was that he had an ulcer on his knee.
As for blancmange, he made it with the best.

CHAUCER
Translated by Nevil Coghill

The Summoner

There was a Summoner with us in the place
Who had a fire-red cherubinny face,
For he had carbuncles. His eyes were narrow,
He was as hot and lecherous as a sparrow.
Black, scabby brows he had, and a thin beard.
Children were afraid when he appeared.
No quicksilver, lead ointments, tartar creams,
Boracic, no, nor brimstone, so it seems,
Could make a salve that had the power to bite,
Clean up or cure his whelks of knobby white
Or purge the pimples sitting on his cheeks.

CHAUCER
Translated by Nevil Coghill

Carl

Nobody has ever seen Carl
when he wasn't smiling.

He grins at cats and hydrants
and a huge, wet, collie-like smile
lights up whenever anybody, no matter who,
speaks to him.

When he's hurt
his smile shrinks a little,
pulls its corners in snugly,
but it doesn't go away.

ALDEN NOWLAN

Follower

My father worked with a horse-plough
His shoulders globed like a full sail strung
Between the shafts and the furrow.
The horses strained at his clicking tongue.

An expert. He would set the wing
And fit the bright steel-pointed sock.
The sod rolled over without breaking.
At the head rig, with a single pluck

Of reins, the sweating team turned round
And back into the land. His eye
Narrowed and angled at the ground,
Mapping the furrow exactly.

I stumbled in his hob-nailed wake,
Fell sometimes on the polished sod;
Sometimes he rode me on his back
Dipping and rising to his plod.

I wanted to grow up and plough,
To close one eye, stiffen my arm:
All I ever did was follow
In his broad shadow round the farm.

I was a nuisance, tripping, falling,
Yapping always. But today
It is my father who keeps stumbling
Behind me and will not go away.

SEAMUS HEANEY

Meeting at Night

The gray sea and the long black land;
And the yellow half-moon large and low;
And the startled little waves that leap
In fiery ringlets from their sleep,
As I gain the cove with pushing prow,
And quench its speed in the slushy sand.
Then a mile of warm sea-scented beach;
Three fields to cross till a farm appears;
A tap at the pane, the quick sharp scratch
And a blue spurt of a lighted match,
And a voice less loud, thro' its joys and fears,
Than the two hearts beating each to each.

ROBERT BROWNING

The Leaden-eyed

Let not young souls be smothered out before
They do quaint deeds and fully flaunt their pride.
It is the world's one crime its babes grow dull,
Its poor are ox-like, limp, and leaden-eyed.
Not that they starve, but starve so dreamlessly;
Not that they sow, but that they seldom reap;
Not that they serve, but have no gods to serve;
Not that they die, but that they die like sheep.

VACHEL LINDSAY

At the Lunch Counter

A girl, fifteen perhaps,
licking her finger-tips,
smoothing splotches
of butter and salt
off her blue pants,
cheek muscles rippling.

Nathan who is blind
sidles to the stool beside her.

They talk, he pompously,
she making faces
he can't see,
telling the boys she isn't serious.

I'm Barbara, she says,
blowing her cheeks out,
wrinkling her forehead,
Fred Ward's Barbara.
I have red hair!

She giggles
since her hair is brown
with aluminum
fishes at the temples.

But he can't see.

Then,
she stiffens and frowns
wanting us to go away
so she can be kind.

ALDEN NOWLAN

Mrs. Reece Laughs

Laughter, with us, is no great undertaking;
A sudden wave that breaks and dies in breaking.
Laughter with Mrs. Reece is much less simple:
It germinates, it spreads, dimple by dimple,
From small beginnings, things of easy girth,
To formidable redundancies of mirth.
Clusters of subterranean chuckles rise,
And presently the circles of her eyes
Close into slits, and all the woman heaves
As a great elm with all its mound of leaves
Wallows before the storm. From hidden sources
A mustering of blind volcanic forces
Takes her and shakes her till she sobs and gapes.
Then all that load of bottled mirth escapes
In one wild crow, a lifting of huge hands,
And creaking stays, a visage that expands
In scarlet ridge and furrow. Thence collapse,
A hanging head, a feeble hand that flaps
An apron-end to stir an air and waft
A streaming face. . . . And Mrs. Reece has laughed.

MARTIN ARMSTRONG

Base Details

If I were fierce and bald and short of breath,
    I'd live with scarlet Majors at the Base,
And speed glum heroes up the line to death.
    You'd see me with my puffy petulant face,
Guzzling and gulping in the best hotel,
    Reading the Roll of Honour. "Poor young chap,"
I'd say—"I used to know his father well.
    Yes, we've lost heavily in this last scrap."
And when the war is done and youth stone dead,
I'd toddle safely home and die—in bed.

SIEGFRIED SASSOON

Mrs. Ogmore-Pritchard

Now, in her iceberg-white, holily laundered crinoline nightgown, under virtuous polar sheets, in her spruced and scoured dust-defying bedroom in trig and trim Bay View, a house for paying guests, at the top of the town, Mrs. Ogmore-Pritchard widow, twice, of Mr. Ogmore, linoleum, retired, and Mr. Pritchard, failed bookmaker, who maddened by besoming, swabbing and scrubbing, the voice of the vacuum-cleaner and the fume of polish, ironically swallowed disinfectant, fidgets in her rinsed sleep, wakes in a dream, and nudges in the ribs dead Mr. Ogmore, dead Mr. Pritchard, ghostly on either side.

MRS. OGMORE-PRITCHARD
Mr. Ogmore!
Mr. Pritchard!
It is time to inhale your balsam.

MR. OGMORE
Oh, Mrs. Ogmore!

MR. PRITCHARD
Oh, Mrs. Pritchard!

MRS. OGMORE-PRITCHARD
Soon it will be time to get up.
Tell me your tasks, in order.

MR. OGMORE
I must put my pyjamas in the drawer marked pyjamas.

MR. PRITCHARD
I must take my cold bath which is good for me.

MR. OGMORE
I must wear my flannel band to ward off sciatica.

MR. PRITCHARD
I must dress behind the curtain and put on my apron.

MR. OGMORE
I must blow my nose.

MRS. OGMORE-PRITCHARD
In the garden, if you please.

MR. OGMORE
In a piece of tissue-paper which I afterwards burn.

MR. PRITCHARD
I must take my salts which are nature's friend.

MR. OGMORE
I must boil the drinking water because of germs.

MR. PRITCHARD
I must make my herb tea which is free from tannin.

MR. OGMORE
And have a charcoal biscuit which is good for me.

MR. PRITCHARD
I may smoke one pipe of asthma mixture.

MRS. OGMORE-PRITCHARD
In the woodshed, if you please.

MR. PRITCHARD
And dust the parlour and spray the canary.

MR. OGMORE
I must put on rubber gloves and search the peke for fleas.

MR. PRITCHARD
I must dust the blinds and then I must raise them.

MRS. OGMORE-PRITCHARD
And before you let the sun in, mind it wipes its shoes.

DYLAN THOMAS

The Song of the Old Mother

I rise in the dawn, and I kneel and blow
Till the seed of the fire flicker and glow;
And then I must scrub and bake and sweep
Till stars are beginning to blink and peep;
And the young lie long and dream in their bed
Of the matching of ribbons for bosom and head,
And their day goes over in idleness,
And they sigh if the wind but lift a tress:
While I must work because I am old,
And the seed of the fire gets feeble and cold.

W. B. YEATS

Flood

The lingering clouds, rolling, rolling,
And the settled rain, dripping, dripping,
In the Eight Directions — the same dusk.
The level lands — one great river.
Wine I have, wine I have:
Idly I drink at the eastern window.
Longingly — I think of my friends,
But neither boat nor carriage comes.

T'AO CH'IEN (A.D. 365-427)

My Parents Kept Me

My parents kept me from children who were rough
Who threw words like stones and who wore torn clothes.
Their thighs showed through rags. They ran in the street
And climbed cliffs and stripped by the country streams.

I feared more than tigers their muscles like iron
Their jerking hands and their knees tight on my arms.
I feared the salt coarse pointing of these boys
Who copied my lisp behind me on the road.

They were lithe, they sprang out behind the hedges
Like dogs to bark at my world. They threw mud
While I looked the other way, pretending to smile.
I longed to forgive them but they never smiled.

STEPHEN SPENDER

The Lamentation of the Old Pensioner

Although I shelter from the rain
Under a broken tree,
My chair was nearest to the fire
In every company
That talked of love or politics,
Ere Time transfigured me.

Though lads are making pikes again
For some conspiracy,
And crazy rascals rage their fill
At human tyranny;
My contemplations are of Time
That has transfigured me.

There's not a woman turns her face
Upon a broken tree,
And yet the beauties that I loved
Are in my memory;
I spit into the face of Time
That has transfigured me.

W. B. YEATS

The Centurion

'What is it now? More trouble?
Another Jew? I might have known it.
These Jews, they buzz around the tail of trouble
Like lascivious flies. Do they think we're here
Because we love them? Is it their climate
That holds us here? Why think, Marcellus—
By God, just dream of it. To-day in Rome,
Less than two thousand thirsty miles away,
Fountains and squares and shaded colonnades,
Men with smooth chins and girls that sometimes wash.

Well, who is it? . . . I see.
Another to be taken to that bonehill.
They're coming now. Just listen to them!—
You'd think they had a dozen there at least.
My sword, Marcellus, I'll be back to dinner,
Unless this fellow's a reluctant dier
Who loves the world too well.
Halt! Stop that shouting. Why is he dressed like that?'
(His robes are purple. On his head
A hedge-crown. Where the thorns are driven
Berries of blood leap up . . .) 'My Orders differ.
Remove that crown—at once—return his clothes.
Kingship can wait until his throne is ready.
Till then, safe conduct. Hold your lines—
Especially that to windward: I've no fondness
For foreign spittle. Hold them. March . . .'
'Halt! Here's the place. Set down the cross.
You three attend to it. And remember, Marcus,
The blows are struck, the nails are driven
For Roman law and Roman order,
Not for your private satisfaction.
Set to work.'
(This grass is bare, sand-coloured: the hill
Quivers with heat.) 'What? As you please.
Seamless?—Then dice for it.' (The sun
Is brutal in this land, metallic.
It works for death, not life.) 'Well, is it done?
Now nail the board above: "King of the Jews."
That turns the mockery on them. Watch them wince
At the superscription. Look, their faces!
Hate, which man is hated most,
Myself or him? He'll serve for both:
They know their limitations. They know,
Greek, Jew or Roman, there is one command,
One only. What's his name?—
He takes it quietly. From Nazareth?

I know it well. Who would exchange it
For this sad city, and become
The food for flies? Marcus there!
Give him some wine: he won't last long.'
That strain of wrist, the arm's tension
And scarecrow hang of chest. 'Ah well,
Poor devil, he's got decent eyes.'

CLIVE SANSOM

Butch Weldy

After I got religion and steadied down
They gave me a job in the canning works,
And every morning I had to fill
The tank in the yard with gasoline,
That fed the blow-fires in the sheds
To heat the soldering irons.
And I mounted a rickety ladder to do it,
Carrying buckets full of the stuff.
One morning, as I stood there pouring,
The air grew still and seemed to heave,
And I shot up as the tank exploded,
And down I came with both legs broken,
And my eyes burned crisp as a couple of eggs.
For someone left a blow-fire going,
And something sucked the flame in the tank.
The Circuit Judge said whoever did it
Was a fellow-servant of mine, and so
Old Rhodes' son didn't have to pay me.
And I sat on the witness stand as blind
As Jack the Fiddler, saying over and over,
"I didn't know him at all."

EDGAR LEE MASTERS

The Man in the Bowler Hat

I am the unnoticed, the unnoticeable man:
The man who sat on your right in the morning train:
The man you looked through like a windowpane:
The man who was the colour of the carriage, the colour of
    the mounting
Morning pipe smoke.

I am the man too busy with a living to live,
Too hurried and worried to see and smell and touch:
The man who is patient too long and obeys too much
And wishes too softly and seldom.

I am the man they call the nation's backbone,
Who am boneless—playable catgut, pliable clay:
The Man they label Little lest one day
I dare to grow.

I am the rails on which the moment passes,
The megaphone for many words and voices:
I am graph, diagram,
Composite face.

I am the led, the easily-fed,
The tool, the not-quite-fool,
The would-be-safe-and-sound,
The uncomplaining, bound,
The dust fine-ground,
Stone-for-a-statue waveworn pebble-round.

A. S. J. TESSIMOND

Solitaire

When night drifts along the streets of the city,
And sifts down between the uneven roofs,
My mind begins to poke and peer.
It plays at ball in odd, blue Chinese gardens,
And shakes wrought dice-cups in Pagan Temples
Amid the broken flutings of white pillars.
It dances with purple and yellow crocuses in its hair,
And its feet shine as they flutter over drenched grasses.
How light and laughing my mind is,
When all good folk have put out their bedroom candles,
And the city is still!

AMY LOWELL

Warren Pryor

When every pencil meant a sacrifice
his parents boarded him at school in town,
slaving to free him from the stony fields,
the meagre acreage that bore them down.

They blushed with pride when, at his graduation,
they watched him picking up the slender scroll,
his passport from the years of brutal toil
and lonely patience in a barren hole.

When he went in the Bank their cups ran over.
They marvelled how he wore a milk-white shirt
work days and jeans on Sundays. He was saved
from their thistle-strewn farm and its red dirt.

And he said nothing. Hard and serious
like a young bear inside his teller's cage,
his axe-hewn hands upon the paper bills
aching with empty strength and throttled rage.

ALDEN NOWLAN

The Evening Wind

The evening wind begins its whistling sound;
The waning moon pours out shining beams.
I love to open the door and gaze idly—
I can stroll slowly if I have a stick.

Little frost, the trees mostly green,
The spring water is flowing through the field ditches.
I remember the days of my childhood,
Playing chess, with a board scrabbled on the ground.

LU YU (A.D. 1125-1209)

Levy Silver

Why did I sell you plated silver,
Rhinestones and synthetic rubies?
Why did I sell you gold-filled cases?
The question at stake is why did you buy?
I couldn't sell them as real and prosper.
But you could buy and pretend them real,
As part of your game of fooling each other
With fake morality, hollow customs,
And laws compounded of spurious stuff.
The goods I sold matched something in you;
For some of your souls were only plated;
And some of you put yourselves together
To imitate virtues clear and precious:
And some of you were mostly brass
Under a film of gold!

EDGAR LEE MASTERS

Autumn Baskets

Old woman cabbage queen
gourd-tapper fortune
hunter in teacups
the black plumes
of your hatboat
quiver in the wind
tremble with secret
piracy as your knowing
hand touches without
gloves the supreme
trophy of the season's
cargo—peppersquash.

When you come home
to your rooming house
with the reddest apple
the most grooved most
crenellated peppersquash
the other old ladies
will vote you the
prize for picking
you will be snow white
and rose red you will
be royal at last
queening it in the
communal kitchen of
your rooming house.

MIRIAM WADDINGTON

To a Fat Lady Seen from the Train

O why do you walk through the fields in gloves,
    Missing so much and so much?
O fat white woman whom nobody loves,
    Why do you walk through the fields in gloves,
When the grass is soft as the breast of doves
    And shivering-sweet to the touch?
O why do you walk through the fields in gloves,
    Missing so much and so much?

FRANCES CORNFORD

My Papa's Waltz

The whiskey on your breath
Could make a small boy dizzy;
But I held on like death:
Such waltzing was not easy.

We romped until the pans
Slid from the kitchen shelf;
My mother's countenance
Could not unfrown itself.

The hand that held my wrist
Was battered on one knuckle;
At every step I missed
My right ear scraped a buckle.

You beat time on my head
With a palm caked hard by dirt,
Then waltzed me off to bed
Still clinging to your shirt.

THEODORE ROETHKE

Farm Scene

The noisy blathering calves are fed, and all
The cows are fothered up and in their stall;
Weary with toils and plodding through the mire,
The ploughmen all are round the kitchen fire;
One pats the shaggy dog between his legs,
Another throws a crust to one that begs;
One sings a song and strokes in highest glee
The tabby cat that sits upon his knee;
One cracks about his horses and his plough,
One kisses Dolly 'cause he milked her cow;
Another has a smutty word to say
And makes the maiden blush and turn away;
Till every song is sung and tale is said,
Then maids lap up the fire and all to bed.

JOHN CLARE

Fireweed (New Brunswick)

Summer is not a season here;
August by the dirt road
ferns and the leaves of bushes brown as beer,
all dead, curdle the blood.

Driving Sunday through woods, I found
one stalk of fireweed, which
was the only live flower in the ground
along twelve miles of ditch.

ALDEN NOWLAN

Digging

To-day I think
Only with scents,—scents dead leaves yield,
And bracken, and wild carrot's seed,
And the square mustard field;

Odours that rise
When the spade wounds the root of tree,
Rose, currant, raspberry, or goutweed,
Rhubarb or celery;

The smoke's smell, too,
Flowing from where a bonfire burns
The dead, the waste, the dangerous,
And all to sweetness turns.

It is enough
To smell, to crumble the dark earth,
While the robin sings over again
Sad songs of Autumn mirth.

EDWARD THOMAS

The Fynch Cows

The Fynch cows poisoned:
they'd torn the fence down,
gored one another for the befouled weed;
next day they bloated
and their bowels bled,
and they staggered crazily
around the miserly pasture—

John Fynch crying
as he stumbled after them,
with his rifle.

ALDEN NOWLAN

The Year

The crocus, while the days are dark,
    Unfolds its saffron sheen;
At April's touch, the crudest bark
    Discovers gems of green.

Then sleep the seasons, full of might;
    While slowly swells the pod
And rounds the peach, and in the night
    The mushroom bursts the sod.

The winter comes: the frozen rut
    Is bound with silver bars;
The snow-drift heaps against the hut;
    And night is pierced with stars.

COVENTRY PATMORE

Tall Nettles

Tall nettles cover up, as they have done
These many springs, the rusty harrow, the plough
Long worn out, and the roller made of stone:
Only the elm butt tops the nettles now.

This corner of the farmyard I like most:
As well as any bloom upon a flower
I like the dust on the nettles, never lost
Except to prove the sweetness of a shower.

EDWARD THOMAS

Early Light

When morning is early, is early,
    the land lies cool
as the delicate floor
    of a limpid pool.

The spires of the churches rise
    from the still green meads,
like tapering fingers
    of water-weeds.

The farms in the fold of the hill,
    and the clear, carved trees,
have sunk to the bottom
    of crystal seas:

have sunk into seas of glass,
    and are drowned so deep
no ripple can shatter
    their shining sleep.

LILIAN BOWES LYON

Winter

Snow wind-whipt to ice
    Under a hard sun:
Stream-runnels curdled hoar
    Crackle, cannot run.

Robin stark dead on twig,
    Song stiffened in it:
Fluffed feathers may not warm
  Bone-thin linnet:

Big-eyed rabbit, lost,
    Scrabbles the snow,
Searching for long-dead grass
    With frost-bit toe:

Mad-tired on the road
    Old Kelly goes;
Through crookt fingers snuffs the air
    Knife-cold in his nose.

Hunger-weak, snow-dazzled,
    Old Thomas Kelly
Thrusts his bit hands, for warmth,
    'Twixt waistcoat and belly.

RICHARD HUGHES

The Storm

First there were two of us, then there were three of us,
Then there was one bird more,
Four of us—wild white sea-birds,
Treading the ocean floor;
And the wind rose, and the sea rose,
To the angry billows' roar—
With one of us—two of us—three of us—four of us
Sea-birds on the shore.

Soon there were five of us, soon there were nine of us,
And lo! in a trice sixteen!
And the yeasty surf curdled over the sands,
The gaunt grey rocks between;
And the tempest raved, and the lightning's fire
Struck blue on the spindrift hoar—
And on four of us—ay, and on four times four of us
Sea-birds on the shore.

And our sixteen waxed to thirty-two,
And they to past three score—
A wild, white welter of winnowing wings,
And ever more and more;
And the winds lulled, and the sea went down,
And the sun streamed out on high,
Gilding the pools and the spume and the spars
'Neath the vast blue deeps of the sky;

And the isles and the bright green headlands shone,
As they'd never shone before,
Mountains and valleys of silver cloud,
Wherein to swing, sweep, soar—
A host of screeching, scolding, scrabbling
Sea-birds on the shore—
A snowy, silent, sun-washed drift
Of sea-birds on the shore.

WALTER DE LA MARE

A Sheep Fair

The day arrives of the autumn fair,
        And torrents fall,
Though sheep in throngs are gathered there,
        Ten thousand all,
Sodden with hurdles round them reared:
        And, lot by lot, the pens are cleared,
        And the auctioneer wrings out his beard,
        And wipes his book, bedrenched and smeared,
And rakes the rain from his face with the edge of his hand,
            As torrents fall.

The wool of the ewes is like a sponge
        With the daylong rain:
Jammed tight, to turn, or lie, or lunge,
        They strive in vain.
        Their horns are soft as finger-nails,
        Their shepherds reek against the rails,
        The tied dogs soak with tucked-in tails,
        The buyers' hat-brims fill like pails,
Which spill small cascades when they shift their stand
      In the daylong rain.

Postscript

Time had trailed lengthily since met
        At Pummery Fair
Those panting thousands in their wet
        And woolly wear:
        And every flock long since has bled,
        And all the dripping buyers have sped,
        And the hoarse auctioneer is dead,
      Who 'Going-going!' so often said,
As he consigned to doom each meek, mewed band
        At Pummery Fair.

THOMAS HARDY

Moonlit Apples

At the top of the house the apples are laid in rows,
And the skylight lets the moonlight in, and those
Apples are deep-sea apples of green. There goes
      A cloud on the moon in the autumn night.

A mouse in the wainscot scratches, and scratches, and then
There is no sound at the top of the house of men
Or mice; and the cloud is blown, and the moon again
      Dapples the apples with deep sea light.

They are lying in rows there, under the gloomy beams;
On the sagging floor; they gather the silver streams
Out of the moon, those moonlit apples of dreams,
    And quiet is the steep stair under.

In the corridors under there is nothing but sleep,
And stiller than ever an orchard bough they keep
Tryst with the moon, and deep is the silence, deep
    On moon-washed apples of wonder.

JOHN DRINKWATER

Pied Beauty

Glory be to God for dappled things—
  For skies of couple-colour as a brinded cow;
    For rose-moles all in stipple upon trout that swim;
Fresh-firecoal chestnut-falls; finches' wings;
  Landscape plotted and pieced—fold, fallow, and plough;
    And all trades, their gear and tackle and trim.

All things counter, original, spare, strange;
  Whatever is fickle, freckled (who knows how?)
    With swift, slow; sweet, sour; adazzle, dim;
He fathers-forth whose beauty is past change:
                    Praise him.

GERARD MANLEY HOPKINS

The Crayfish

I

The brook wound through the woods behind
The houses, on each trim side was lined
With a wall of orange-brown rocks.
There, I sat with my shoes and socks
Off, under the tall oaks on the bank,
And dangled a piece of string that sank
Its load of bacon slowly down
To the dusty bottom. No sound
Ruffled the water, when I saw
A big crayfish stepping near the raw
Bait. I moved the string to inform
Him of it—back he leaped in a storm
Of cloudy mud. But soon he returned
Clumsy to eat what he had learned
Was easy lunch. He paused to fondle
The soggy dish, then like a bundle
Took it in his heavy pincers. Up,
Up, carefully I drew him up,
Dripping, through his watery sky,
Into my world of green and dry.

II

He started off with a waddling walk
From the ledge, but wanting to talk
I set him back. So he sat there,
His black-reflector eyes in a stare
Of strangeness, while I told and told
How I was a boy, was nine years old,
And liked him. He swayed his feelers round
To show attention at the sound
I made, in the hollow glade of noon.

Wet slow scrapings were all the tune
His clumsy pincers could provide
For answer. I stroked his armoured side,
Brown with yellow speckles like hail
In a dry garden, his plated tail
With its fan-feather tips, his spiny
Spider-legs (one missing): my tiny
Monster from the stream. And to show
How well I liked him I let him go.

III

I dropped him back with a soft splash
To catch again, and in a flash
He shot away in his liquid world
Between two rocks. Slowly I unfurled
My string, and let the tattered bait
Down into his sky again, to wait
On the dusty bottom. The string
Sent wrinkles out in widening rings,
That touched against the wall to go
Sliding back like messengers to and fro,
To confuse the sun. Mottled in shade
And sun the stream moved its slow parade
Between the walls; the watery bed
Lay like a desert rock-strewn and dead
Around my line. I'd thought to hoist
My brown acquaintance up from his moist
Nook beneath the rocks, to let him eat
The bacon as a friendly treat.
Below, I could see his pointed snout
Watching, but nothing would coax him out
To ride again up the sunny air.
I had to go and leave him there.

ROBERT WALLACE

The Heron

The heron stands in water where the swamp
Has deepened to the blackness of a pool,
Or balances with one leg on a hump
Of marsh grass heaped above a muskrat hole.

He walks the shallow with an antic grace.
The great feet break the ridges of the sand,
The long eye notes the minnow's hiding place.
His beak is quicker than a human hand.

He jerks a frog across his bony lip,
Then points his heavy bill above the wood.
The wide wings flap but once to lift him up.
A single ripple starts from where he stood.

THEODORE ROETHKE

The Fish

I caught a tremendous fish
and held him beside the boat
half out of water, with my hook
fast in a corner of his mouth.
He didn't fight.
He hadn't fought at all.

He hung a grunting weight,
battered and venerable
and homely. Here and there
his brown skin hung in strips
like ancient wallpaper,
and its pattern of darker brown
was like wallpaper:
shapes like full-blown roses
stained and lost through age.
He was speckled with barnacles,
fine rosettes of lime,
and infested
with tiny white sea-lice,
and underneath two or three
rags of green weed hung down.
While his gills were breathing in
the terrible oxygen
—the frightening gills
fresh and crisp with blood,
that can cut so badly—
I thought of the coarse white flesh
packed in like feathers,
the big bones and the little bones,
the dramatic reds and blacks
of his shiny entrails,
and the pink swim-bladder
like a big peony.
I looked into his eyes
which were far larger than mine
but shallower, and yellowed,
the iris backed and packed
with tarnished tinfoil
seen through the lenses
of old scratched isinglass.
They shifted a little, but not
to return my stare.

—It was more like the tipping
of an object toward the light.
I admired his sullen face,
the mechanism of his jaw,
and then I saw
that from his lower lip
—if you could call it a lip—
grim, wet, and weapon-like,
hung five old pieces of fish-line,
or four and a wire leader
with the swivel still attached,
with all their five big hooks
grown firmly in his mouth.
A green line, frayed at the end
where he broke it, two heavier lines
and a fine black thread
still crimped from the strain and snap
when it broke and he got away.
Like medals with their ribbons
frayed and wavering,
a five-haired beard of wisdom
trailing from his aching jaw.
I stared and stared
and victory filled up
the little rented boat,
from the pool of bilge
where oil had spread a rainbow
around the rusted engine
to the bailer rusted orange,
the sun-cracked thwarts,
the oarlocks on their strings,
the gunnels—until everything
was rainbow, rainbow, rainbow!
And I let the fish go.

ELIZABETH BISHOP

The Pool in the Rock

In this water, clear as air,
Lurks a lobster in its lair.
Rock-bound weed sways out and in,
Coral-red, and bottle-green.
Wondrous pale anemones
Stir like flowers in a breeze:
Fluted scallop, whelk in shell,
And the prowling mackerel.
Winged with snow the sea-mews ride
The brine-keen wind; and far and wide
Sounds on the hollow thunder of the tide.

WALTER DE LA MARE

Mountain Lion

Climbing through the January snow, into the Lobo
canyon
Dark grow the spruce-trees, blue is the balsam, water
sounds still unfrozen, and the trail is still evident.

Men!
Two men!
Men! The only animal in the world to fear!

They hesitate.
We hesitate.
They have a gun.
We have no gun.

Then we all advance, to meet.

Two Mexicans, strangers, emerging out of the dark
    and snow and inwardness of the Lobo valley.
What are you doing here on this vanishing trail?

What is he carrying?
Something yellow.
A deer?

¿ Qué tiene, amigo?
León—

He smiles, foolishly, as if he were caught doing wrong.
And we smile, foolishly, as if we didn't know.
He is quite gentle and dark-faced.

It is a mountain lion,
A long, long slim cat, yellow like a lioness.
Dead.
He trapped her this morning, he says, smiling foolishly.

Lift up her face,
Her round, bright face, bright as frost.
Her round, fine-fashioned head, with two dead ears;
And stripes in the brilliant frost of her face, sharp, fine
    dark rays,
Dark, keen, fine eyes in the brilliant frost of her face.
Beautiful dead eyes.

¡ Hermoso es!

They go out towards the open;
We go on into the gloom of Lobo.
And above the trees I found her lair,
A hole in the blood-orange brilliant rocks that stick up,
    a little cave.
And bones, and twigs, and a perilous ascent.

So, she will never leap up that way again, with the yellow
flash of a mountain lion's long shoot!
And her bright striped frost-face will never watch any more,
out of the shadow of the cave in the blood-orange rock,
Above the trees of the Lobo dark valley-mouth!
Instead, I look out.
And out to the dim of the desert, like a dream, never
real;

To the snow of the Sangre de Cristo mountains, the ice
of the mountains of Picoris,
And near across at the opposite steep of snow, green trees
motionless standing in snow, like a Christmas toy.

And I think in this empty world there was room for me
and a mountain lion.
And I think in the world beyond, how easily we might
spare a million or two of humans
And never miss them.
Yet what a gap in the world, the missing white frost-face
of that slim yellow mountain lion!

D. H. LAWRENCE

A Narrow Fellow

A narrow fellow in the grass
Occasionally rides;
You may have met him,—did you not?
His notice sudden is.

The grass divides as with a comb,
A spotted shaft is seen;
And then it closes at your feet
And opens further on.

He likes a boggy acre,
A floor too cool for corn.
Yet when a child, and barefoot,
I more than once, at morn,

Have passed, I thought, a whip-lash
Unbraiding in the sun,—
When, stopping to secure it,
It wrinkled, and was gone.

Several of nature's people
I know, and they know me;
I feel for them a transport
Of cordiality;

But never met this fellow,
Attended or alone,
Without a tighter breathing,
And zero at the bone.

EMILY DICKINSON

The Donkey

When fishes flew and forests walked,
    And figs grew upon thorn,
Some moment when the moon was blood,
    Then surely I was born.

With monstrous head and sickening cry
    And ears like errant wings,
The devil's walking parody
    On all four-footed things.

The tattered outlaw of the earth,
    Of ancient crooked will;
Starve, scourge, deride me: I am dumb,
    I keep my secret still.

Fools! For I also had my hour;
    One far fierce hour and sweet:
There was a shout about my ears,
    And palms before my feet.

G. K. CHESTERTON

The Flower-fed Buffaloes

The flower-fed buffaloes of the spring
In the days of long ago,
Ranged where the locomotives sing
And the prairie flowers lie low;—
The tossing, blooming, perfumed grass
Is swept away by the wheat,
Wheels and wheels and wheels spin by
In the spring that still is sweet.
But the flower-fed buffaloes of the spring
Left us, long ago.
They gore no more, they bellow no more,
They trundle around the hills no more:—
With the Blackfeet, lying low,
With the Pawnees, lying low
Lying low.

VACHEL LINDSAY

The Zoo

I scarcely think
    I like the Zoo
as much as other
    people do.

First when I see
    the elephants,
they seem in trouble
    with their pants,

and when the hippo-
    potamus
says, "Who in blazes
    made me thus?"

And I observe the
    chimpanzee
thanking his God
    he's not like me.

While all varieties
    of cat,
make me feel dumpy,
    coarse and fat.

And that's not all!
    The eagles make
me stare as though
    my heart would break

at the great spaces
    of the air.
And why? It isn't
    my affair

if a hippo is a
    sort of evil
joke perpetrated
    by the devil,

and of all broken-
    hearted things
the brokenest are
    captive wings!

And yet I can-
    not like the Zoo
as much as other
    people do.

HUMBERT WOLFE

Snake

A snake came to my water-trough
On a hot, hot day, and I in pyjamas for the heat,
To drink there.

In the deep, strange-scented shade of the great dark
    carob-tree
I came down the steps with my pitcher
And must wait, must stand and wait, for there he was
    at the trough before me.

He reached down from a fissure in the earth-wall in the
    gloom
And trailed his yellow-brown slackness soft-bellied
    down, over the edge of the stone trough
And rested his throat upon the stone bottom,
And where the water had dripped from the tap, in a
    small clearness,
He sipped with his straight mouth,
Softly drank through his straight gums, into his slack
    long body,
Silently.

Someone was before me at my water-trough,
And I, like a second comer, waiting.

He lifted his head from his drinking, as cattle do,
And looked at me vaguely, as drinking cattle do,
And flickered his two-forked tongue from his lips and, mused a moment,
And stooped and drank a little more,
Being earth-brown, earth-golden from the burning bowels of the earth
On the day of Sicilian July, with Etna smoking.

The voice of my education said to me
He must be killed,
For in Sicily the black, black snakes are innocent, the gold are venomous.

And voices in me said, If you were a man
You would take a stick and break him now, and finish him off.

But must I confess how I liked him,
How glad I was he had come like a guest in quiet, to drink at my water-trough
And depart peaceful, pacified, and thankless,
Into the burning bowels of this earth?

Was it cowardice, that I dared not kill him?
Was it perversity, that I longed to talk to him?
Was it humility, to feel so honoured?
I felt so honoured.

And yet those voices:
If you were not afraid, you would kill him!

And truly I was afraid, I was most afraid,
But even so, honoured still more
That he should seek my hospitality
From out the dark door of the secret earth.

He drank enough
And lifted his head, dreamily, as one who has drunken,
And flickered his tongue like a forked night on the air,
so black,
Seeming to lick his lips,
And looked around like a god, unseeing, into the air,
And slowly turned his head,
And slowly, very slowly, as if thrice adream,
Proceeded to draw his slow length curving round
And climb again the broken bank of my wall-face.

And as he put his head into that dreadful hole,
And as he slowly drew up, snake-easing his shoulders,
and entered farther,
A sort of horror, a sort of protest against his withdrawing
into that horrid black hole,
Deliberately going into the blackness, and slowly drawing
himself after,
Overcame me now his back was turned.

I looked round, I put down my pitcher,
I picked up a clumsy log
And threw it at the water-trough with a clatter.

I think it did not hit him,
But suddenly that part of him that was left behind convulsed
in undignified haste,
Writhed like lightning, and was gone
Into the black hole, the earth-lipped fissure in the wall-
front,
At which, in the intense still noon, I stared with fascination.

And immediately I regretted it.
I thought how paltry, how vulgar, what a mean act!
I despised myself and the voices of my accursed human
education.
And I thought of the albatross,
And I wished he would come back, my snake.

For he seemed to me again like a king,
Like a king in exile, uncrowned in the underworld,
Now due to be crowned again.

And so, I missed my chance with one of the lords
Of life.
And I have something to expiate;
A pettiness.

D. H. LAWRENCE

from

A Bestiary

Deer

Deer are gentle and graceful
And they have beautiful eyes.
They hurt no one but themselves,
The males, and only for love.
Men have invented several
Thousand ways of killing them.

Lion

The lion is called the king
Of beasts. Nowadays there are
Almost as many lions
In cages as out of them.
If offered a crown, refuse.

KENNETH REXROTH

The Buck in the Snow

White sky, over the hemlocks bowed with snow,
Saw you not at the beginning of evening the antlered buck
    and his doe
Standing in the apple-orchard? I saw them. I saw them
    suddenly go,
Tails up, with long leaps lovely and slow,
Over the stone-wall into the wood of hemlocks bowed with
    snow.

Now lies he here, his wild blood scalding the snow.
How strange a thing is death, bringing to his knees,
    bringing to his antlers
The buck in the snow.
How strange a thing,—a mile away by now, it may be,
Under the heavy hemlocks that as the moments pass
Shift their loads a little, letting fall a feather of snow—
Life, looking out attentive from the eyes of the doe.

EDNA ST. VINCENT MILLAY

The Best Beast of the Fat Stock Show at Earl's Court

The Best Beast of the Show
Is fat
He goes by the lift
They all do that.

This lift, large as a room
(Yet the beasts bunch)
Goes up with a groan
They have not oiled the winch

Not yet to the lift
Goes the Best Beast
He has to walk on the floor
To make a show first

Great are his horns
Long his fur
The Beast came from the North
To walk here

Is he not fat?
Is he not fit?
Now in a crown he walks
To the lift

When he lay in his pen
In the close heat
His head lolled, his eyes
Were not shut for sleep.

Slam the lift door
Push it up with a groan
Will they kill the beast now?
Where has he gone?

When he lay in the straw
His heart beat so fast
His hide heaved, I touched his hide
As I walked past.

I touched his hide
I touched the root of his horns
The breath of the Beast
Came in low moans.

STEVIE SMITH

The Crabs

There was a bucket full of them. They spilled,
crawled, climbed, clawed : slowly tossed
and fell : precision made : cold iodine color of their own
world of sand and occasional brown weed, round stone
chilled clean in the chopping waters of their coast.
One fell out. The marine thing on the grass
tried to trundle off, barbarian and immaculate and to be
    killed
with his kin. We lit water : dumped the living mass
in : contemplated tomatoes and corn : and with the good
    cheer of civilized man,
cigarettes, that is, and cold beer, and chatter,
waited out and lived down the ten-foot-away clatter
of crabs as they died for us inside their boiling can.

RICHMOND LATTIMORE

The Bull Moose

Down from the purple mist of trees on the mountain,
lurching through forests of white spruce and cedar,
stumbling through tamarack swamps,
came the bull moose
to be stopped at last by a pole-fenced pasture.

Too tired to turn or, perhaps, aware
there was no place left to go, he stood with the cattle.
They, scenting the musk of death, seeing his great head
like the ritual mask of a blood god, moved to the other end
of the field, and waited.

The neighbours heard of it, and by afternoon
cars lined the road. The children teased him
with alder switches and he gazed at them
like an old, tolerant collie. The women asked
if he could have escaped from a Fair.

The oldest man in the parish remembered seeing
a gelded moose yoked with an ox for plowing.
The young men snickered and tried to pour beer
down his throat while their girl friends took their pictures.

And the bull moose let them stroke his tick-ravaged flanks,
let them pry open his jaws with bottles, let a giggling girl
plant a little purple cap
of thistles on his head.

When the wardens came, everyone agreed it was a shame
to shoot anything so shaggy and cuddlesome.
He looked like the kind of pet
women put to bed with their sons.

So they held their fire. But just as the sun dropped in the river
the bull moose gathered his strength
like a scaffolded king, straightened, and lifted his horns
so that even the wardens backed away as they raised their rifles.
When he roared, people ran to their cars. All the young men
leaned on their automobile horns as he toppled.

ALDEN NOWLAN

Cargoes

Quinquireme of Nineveh from distant Ophir
Rowing home to haven in sunny Palestine,
With a cargo of ivory,
And apes and peacocks,
Sandalwood, cedarwood, and sweet white wine.

Stately Spanish galleon coming from the Isthmus,
Dipping through the Tropics by the palm-green shores,
With a cargo of diamonds,
Emeralds, amethysts,
Topazes, and cinnamon, and gold moidores.

Dirty British coaster with a salt-caked smoke-stack
Butting through the Channel in the mad March days,
With a cargo of Tyne coal,
Road-rail, pig-lead,
Firewood, iron-ware, and cheap tin-trays.

JOHN MASEFIELD

An Old Song Re-sung

I saw a ship a-sailing, a-sailing, a-sailing,
With emeralds and rubies and sapphires in her hold;
And a bosun in a blue coat bawling at the railing,
Piping through a silver call that had a chain of gold;
The summer wind was failing and the tall ship rolled.

I saw a ship a-steering, a-steering, a-steering,
With roses in red thread worked upon her sails;
With sacks of purple amethysts, the spoils of buccaneering,
Skins of musky yellow wine, and silks in bales,
His merry men were cheering, hauling on the brails.

I saw a ship a-sinking, a-sinking, a-sinking,
With glittering sea-water splashing on her decks,
With seamen in her spirit-room singing songs and drinking,
Pulling claret bottles down, and knocking off the necks,
The broken glass was chinking as she sank among the wrecks.

JOHN MASEFIELD

The Skaters

Black swallows swooping or gliding
In a flurry of entangled loops and curves;
The skaters skim over the frozen river.
And the grinding click of their skates as they impinge upon the
surface,
Is like the brushing together of thin wing-tips of silver.

JOHN GOULD FLETCHER

Death

Old Chang died after three years' sickness;
Old Wu suddenly went out one night.
My body is hard like steel.
I lean on the door, gazing at the green hill.

LU YU (1125-1209)

Plucking the Rushes

(A boy and girl are sent to gather rushes for thatching)

Green rushes with red shoots,
Long leaves bending to the wind—
You and I in the same boat
Plucking rushes at the Five Lakes.
We started at dawn from the orchid-island:
We rested under the elms till noon.
You and I plucking the rushes
Had not plucked a handful when night came!

ANONYMOUS (fourth century)
Translated by Arthur Waley

The Red Wheelbarrow

so much depends
upon

a red wheel
barrow

glazed with rain
water

beside the white
chickens.

WILLIAM CARLOS WILLIAMS

Poem

As the cat
climbed over
the top of

the jamcloset
first the right
forefoot

carefully
then the hind
stepped down

into the pit of
the empty
flowerpot.

WILLIAM CARLOS WILLIAMS

Homebrew

Molasses, oranges and yeast
purchased with promises and mixed at night,
the keg buried in steaming dung
to hasten fermentation, then the wait
for some excuse to fork it out
(a rainy day, the mill not running);
the men in their sawdust-covered denims
sitting on blocks of pressed hay in the barn
and drinking from a single mug, their thumbs
spooning out shreds of hay and frequently
flies and then bolting it, holding their breath,
and spitting afterwards, grunting their pleasure.

ALDEN NOWLAN

This Is Just to Say

I have eaten
the plums
that were in
the icebox

and which
you were probably
saving
for breakfast

Forgive me
they were delicious
so sweet
and so cold.

WILLIAM CARLOS WILLIAMS

Eight Haiku

Autumn Nightfall

On a withered branch
a crow has settled—
autumn nightfall.

MATSUA BASHO (1644-1694)

The Barley Field

Up the barley rows
stitching, stitching them together,
a butterfly goes.

SORA (1648-1710)

Autumn Storms

First of all,
it's scarecrows they blow down—
storm-winds of fall!

KYOROKU (1656-1715)

The Short Night

The short night is through:
on the hairy caterpillar,
little beads of dew.

TANIGUCHI BUSON (1715-1783)

The Sudden Chillness

The piercing chill I feel:
my dead wife's comb, in our bedroom,
under my heel . . . .

TANIGUCHI BUSON (1715-1783)

In My Host's Garden

"Don't break it!" he said,
then broke off and gave me
a branch of his plum.

TAIGI (d. 1771)

Spring

Snow melts,
and the village is overflowing—
with children.

ISSA (1762-1826)

Medieval Scene

Eleven of them go,
horsemen who do not turn their heads—
through the wind-blown snow.

MASAOKA SHIKI (1867-1902)

Flute Music

(from *Six Variations*)

two flutes! How close
to each other they move
in mazing figures,
never touching, never
breaking the measure,
as gnats dance in
summer haze all afternoon, over
shallow water sprinkled
with mottled blades of willow—
two flutes!

DENISE LEVERTOV

Three Poems from the Japanese

I

I passed by the beach
At Tago and saw
The snow falling, pure white,
High on the peak of Fuji.

II

The mists rise over
The still pools at Asuka.
Memory does not
Pass away so easily.

III

I wish I were close
To you as the wet skirt of
A salt girl to her body.
I think of you always.

YAMABE NO AKAHITO
Translated by Kenneth Rexroth

Verses

Clean is the autumn wind,
Splendid the autumn moon.
The brown leaves are heaped and scattered,
The ice-cold raven starts from its roost.
Dreaming of you—when shall I see you again?
On this night sorrow fills my heart.

LI PO (A.D. 702?-762)

Verses

You who come from the old village—
Tell me what is happening there.
When you left, were the chill plum blossoms
Flowering beneath the white window?

WANG WEI (A.D. 699-759)

The Cold Mountain

The cold mountain turns dark green.
The autumn stream flows murmuring on.
Leaning on my staff beneath the wicket gate,
In the rushing wind I hear the cry of the aged cicada.

WANG WEI (A.D. 699-759)

The Two Corbies

As I was walking all alone,
I heard two corbies talking:
The one unto the other said,
'Where shall we go and dine today?'

'In behind that old sod dike,
I know there lies a new-slain knight;
And nobody knows that he lies there,
But his hawk, his hound, and lady fair.

'His hound is to the hunting gone,
His hawk to fetch the wild-fowl home,
His lady took another mate,
So we may make our dinner sweet.

'You sit on his fine white neck,
And I'll pick out his pretty blue eye,
With a lock of his golden hair
We'll line our nest when it grows bare.

'Many a one for him does mourn,
But none shall know where he has gone:
O'er his white bones, when they are bare,
The wind shall blow for evermore.'

ANONYMOUS
(Modernized version)

The Leaden Echo

How to keep—is there any any, is there none such, nowhere
known some, bow or brooch or braid or brace, lace, latch
or catch or key to keep
Back beauty, keep it, beauty, beauty, beauty, . . . from vanishing
away?
O is there no frowning of these wrinkles, ranked wrinkles deep,
Down? no waving off of these most mournful messengers, still
messengers, sad and stealing messengers of grey?
No there's none, there's none, O no there's none,
Nor can you long be, what you now are, called fair,
Do what you may do, what, do what you may,
And wisdom is early to despair:
Be beginning; since, no, nothing can be done to keep at bay
Age and age's evils, hoar hair,
Ruck and wrinkle, drooping, dying, death's worst, winding
sheets, tombs and worms and tumbling to decay;
So be beginning, be beginning to despair.
O there's none; no no no there's none:
Be beginning to despair, to despair,
Despair, despair, despair, despair.

GERARD MANLEY HOPKINS

Blue is the smoke of war, white the bones of men.

TU FU (713-770)

Bombing Casualties in Spain

Dolls' faces are rosier but these were children
their eyes not glass but gleaming gristle
dark lenses in whose quicksilvery glances
the sunlight quivered. These blenched lips
were warm once and bright with blood
but blood
held in a moist bleb of flesh
not spilt and spatter'd in tousled hair.

In these shadowy tresses
red petals did not always
thus clot and blacken to a scar.
These are dead faces.
Wasps' nests are not so wanly waxen
wood embers not so greyly ashen.

They are laid out in ranks
like paper lanterns that have fallen
after a night of riot
extinct in the dry morning air.

HERBERT READ

Giorno Dei Morti

Along the avenue of cypresses,
All in their scarlet cloaks and surplices
Of linen, go the chanting choristers,
The priests in gold and black, the villagers.

And all along the path to the cemetery
The round dark heads of men crowd silently,
And black-scarved faces of womenfolk, wistfully
Watch at the banner of death, and the mystery.

And at the foot of a grave a father stands
With sunken head, and forgotten, folded hands;
And at the foot of a grave a mother kneels
With pale shut face, nor either hears nor feels

The coming of the chanting choristers
Between the avenues of cypresses,
The silence of the many villagers,
The candle-flames beside the surplices.

D. H. LAWRENCE

Two Children

Two children, branches of the same tree of wretchedness,
together in a doorway, beneath the torrid night,
two beggar children, covered with sores,
are eating from the same tin, like hungry dogs,
the food cast up by the tide of the tablecloths.
Two children: one black, the other white.

Their heads, pressed together, are sown with lice;
their bare feet, closely joined;
their mouths, tireless in an identical frenzy of jaws;
and above the sour and greasy food,
two hands: one black, the other white.

What a powerful and sincere union!
They are bound by their hunger and by sullen nights,
and by melancholy afternoons in the gleaming avenues,
and by explosive mornings
when the day awakens with its alcoholic eyes.

They are side by side like two good dogs . . .
Together thus, like two good dogs,
one black, the other white,
when the hour of marching comes
will they march as well, like two good men,
one black, the other white?

Two children, branches of the same tree of wretchedness,
are in a doorway, beneath the torrid night.

NICOLAS GUILLÉN (Cuba)
Translated from the Spanish by H. R. Hays

The Responsibility

I am the man who gives the word,
If it should come, to use the Bomb.

I am the man who spreads the word
From him to them if it should come.

I am the man who gets the word
From him who spreads the word from him.

I am the man who drops the Bomb
If ordered by the one who's heard
From him who merely spreads the word
The first one gives if it should come.

I am the man who loads the Bomb
That he must drop should orders come
From him who gets the word passed on
By one who waits to hear from *him*.

I am the man who makes the Bomb
That he must load for him to drop
If told by one who gets the word
From one who passes it from *him*.

I am the man who fills the till,
Who pays the tax, who foots the bill
That guarantees the Bomb he makes
For him to load for him to drop
If orders come from one who gets
The word passed on to him by one
Who waits to hear it from the man
Who gives the word to use the Bomb.

I am the man behind it all;
I am the one responsible.

PETER APPLETON

The Punching Clock

There will come a day
when the punching clock
will no longer just wait in the doorway

it will come directly to our beds
and will ask politely
that we punch our good morning

then it will accompany us
like a courteous servant would
and punch:

when we start to yawn
when we bite into a sandwich
when we think of women
when we think of old age . . .

how wonderful will it be
to have one's whole life punched by seconds
up to the very end. . . .

MILOS MACOUREK
Translated from the Czech by Michael J. Flach

All that's Past

Very old are the woods;
        And the buds that break
Out of the brier's boughs,
When March winds wake,
So old with their beauty are—
        Oh, no man knows
Through what wild centuries
        Roves back the rose.

Very old are the brooks;
        And the rills that rise
Where snow sleeps cold beneath
        The azure skies
Sing such a history
        Of come and gone,
Their every drop is as wise
        As Solomon.

Very old are we men;
        Our dreams are tales
Told in dim Eden
        By Eve's nightingales;
We wake and whisper awhile,
        But, the day gone by,
Silence and sleep like fields
        Of amaranth lie.

WALTER DE LA MARE

The Circus; or One View of It

Said the circus man, Oh what do you like
Best of all about my show—
The circular rings, three rings in a row,
With animals going around, around,
Tamed to go running round, around,
And around, round, around they go;
Or perhaps you like the merry-go-round,
Horses plunging sedately up,
Horses sedately plunging down,
Going around the merry-go-round;
Or perhaps you like the clown with a hoop,
Shouting, rolling the hoop around;
Or the elephants walking around in a ring
Each trunk looped to a tail's loop,
Loosely ambling around the ring;
How do you like this part of the show?

Everything's busy and on the go;
The peanut men cry out and sing,
The round fat clown rolls on the ground,
The trapeze ladies sway and swing,
The circus horses plunge around
The circular rings, three rings in a row;
Here they come, and here they go.
And here you sit, said the circus man,
Around in a circle to watch my show;
Which is show and which is you,
Now that we're here in this circus show,
Do I know? Do you know?
But hooray for the clowns, and the merry-go-round,
The painted horses plunging round,
The live, proud horses stamping the ground,
And the clowns and the elephants swinging around;
Come to my show; hooray for the show,
Hooray for the circus all the way round!
Said the round exuberant circus man.
Hooray for the show! said the circus man.

THEODORE SPENCER

from

Inscriptions at the City of Brass

I

Enter and learn the story of the rulers,
They rested a little in the shadow of my towers
And then they passed.
They were dispersed like those shadows
When the sun goes down;
They were driven like straws
Before the wind of death.

II

The drunkenness of youth has passed like a fever,
And yet I saw many things,
Seeing my glory in the days of my glory.
The feet of my war-horse
Drummed upon the cities of the world,
I sacked great towns like a hot wind
And fell like thunder upon far lands.
The kings of the earth were dragged behind my chariot
And the people of the earth behind my laws;
But now
The drunkenness of youth has passed like a fever,
Like foam upon sand.
Death took me in a net:
My armies warred against him in vain,
My courtiers flattered him in vain.
Listen, O Wayfarer, to the words of my death,
For they were not the words of my life:
Save up your soul
And taste the beautiful wine of peace,
For tomorrow the earth shall answer:
He is with me,
My jealous breast holds him for ever.

III

About this table
Sat many hawk-eyed kings
With many one-eyed kings
To bear them company;
But now all sit in the dark and none are able
None are able to see.

E. POWYS MATHERS
Translated from the Medieval Arabic

Captain Cat

Captain Cat, the retired blind seacaptain, asleep in his bunk in the seashelled, ship-in-bottled, shipshape best cabin of Schooner House dreams of

SECOND VOICE

never such seas as any that swamped the decks of his S.S. Kidwelly bellying over the bedclothes and jellyfish-slippery sucking him down salt deep into the Davy dark where the fish come biting out and nibble him down to his wishbone, and the long drowned nuzzle up to him.

FIRST DROWNED

Remember me, Captain?

CAPTAIN CAT

You're Dancing Williams!

FIRST DROWNED

I lost my step in Nantucket.

SECOND DROWNED

Do you see me, Captain? the white bone talking? I'm Tom-Fred the donkeyman . . .

THIRD DROWNED

Hold me, Captain, I'm Jonah Jarvis, come to a bad end, very enjoyable.

FOURTH DROWNED

Alfred Pomeroy Jones, sea-lawyer, born in Mumbles, sung like a linnet, crowned you with a flagon, tattoed with mermaids, thirst like a dredger, died of blisters.

FIRST DROWNED

This skull at your earhole is

FIFTH DROWNED

Curly Bevan. Tell my auntie it was me that pawned the ormolu clock.

CAPTAIN CAT

Aye, aye, Curly.

SECOND DROWNED

Tell my missus no I never

THIRD DROWNED

I never done what she said I never.

FOURTH DROWNED

Yes they did.

FIFTH DROWNED

And who brings coconuts and shawls and parrots to *my* Gwen now?

FIRST DROWNED

How's it above?

SECOND DROWNED

Is there rum and laverbread?

THIRD DROWNED

Bosoms and robins?

FOURTH DROWNED

Concertinas?

FIFTH DROWNED

Ebenezer's bell?

FIRST DROWNED

Fighting and onions?

SECOND DROWNED
And sparrows and daisies?

THIRD DROWNED
Tiddlers in a jamjar?

FOURTH DROWNED
Buttermilk and whippets?

FIFTH DROWNED
Rock-a-bye baby?

FIRST DROWNED
Washing on the line?

SECOND DROWNED
And old girls in the snug?

THIRD DROWNED
How's the tenors in Dowlais?

FOURTH DROWNED
Who milks the cows in Maesgwyn?

FIFTH DROWNED
When she smiles, is there dimples?

FIRST DROWNED
What's the smell of parsley?

CAPTAIN CAT
Oh, my dead dears!

DYLAN THOMAS

Dulce Et Decorum Est

Bent double, like old beggars under sacks,
Knock-kneed, coughing like hags, we cursed through sludge,
Till on the haunting flares we turned our backs,
And towards our distant rest began to trudge.
Men marched asleep. Many had lost their boots,
But limped on, blood-shod. All went lame, all blind;
Drunk with fatigue; deaf even to the hoots
Of gas-shells dropping softly behind.

Gas! GAS! Quick, boys!—An ecstasy of fumbling,
Fitting the clumsy helmets just in time,
But someone still was yelling out and stumbling
And floundering like a man in fire or lime.—
Dim through the misty panes and thick green light,
As under a green sea, I saw him drowning.

In all my dreams before my helpless sight
He plunges at me, guttering, choking, drowning.

If in some smothering dreams, you too could pace
Behind the wagon that we flung him in,
And watch the white eyes writhing in his face,
His hanging face, like a devil's sick of sin,
If you could hear, at every jolt, the blood
Come gargling from the froth-corrupted lungs
Bitter as the cud
Of vile, incurable sores on innocent tongues,—
My friend, you would not tell with such high zest
To children ardent for some desperate glory,
The old Lie: Dulce et decorum est
Pro patria mori.

WILFRED OWEN

Acquainted with the Night

I have been one acquainted with the night.
I have walked out in rain—and back in rain.
I have outwalked the furthest city light.

I have looked down the saddest city lane,
I have passed by the watchman on his beat
And dropped my eyes, unwilling to explain.

I have stood still and stopped the sound of feet
When far away an interrupted cry
Came over houses from another street,

But not to call me back or say good-bye;
And further still at an unearthly height,
One luminary clock against the sky

Proclaimed the time was neither wrong nor right.
I have been one acquainted with the night.

ROBERT FROST

O What Is that Sound?

O what is that sound which so thrills the ear
    Down in the valley drumming, drumming?
Only the scarlet soldiers, dear,
    The soldiers coming.

O what is that light I see flashing so clear
    Over the distance brightly, brightly?
Only the sun on their weapons, dear,
    As they step lightly.

O what are they doing with all that gear,
    What are they doing this morning, this morning?
Only their usual manoeuvres, dear,
    Or perhaps a warning.

O why have they left the road down there,
    Why are they suddenly wheeling, wheeling?
Perhaps a change in their orders, dear.
    Why are you kneeling?

O haven't they stopped for the doctor's care,
    Haven't they reined their horses, their horses?
Why, they are none of them wounded, dear,
    None of these forces.

O is it the parson they want, with white hair,
    Is it the parson, is it, is it?
No, they are passing his gateway, dear,
    Without a visit.

O it must be the farmer who lives so near.
    It must be the farmer so cunning, so cunning?
They have passed the farmyard already, dear,
    And now they are running.

O where are you going? Stay with me here!
    Were the vows you swore deceiving, deceiving?
No, I promised to love you, dear,
    But I must be leaving.

O it's broken the lock and splintered the door,
    O it's the gate where they're turning, turning;
Their boots are heavy on the floor
    And their eyes are burning.

W. H. AUDEN

Counter-attack

We'd gained our first objective hours before
While dawn broke like a face with blinking eyes,
Pallid, unshaved and thirsty, blind with smoke.
Things seemed all right at first. We held their line,
With bombers posted, Lewis guns well placed,
And clink of shovels deepening the shallow trench.
    The place was rotten with dead; green clumsy legs
    High-booted, sprawled and grovelled along the saps
    And trunks, face downward, in the sucking mud,
    Wallowed like trodden sand-bags loosely filled;
    And naked sodden buttocks, mats of hair,
    Bulged, clotted heads slept in the plastering slime.
    And then the rain began,—the jolly old rain!

A yawning soldier knelt against the bank,
Staring across the morning blear with fog;
He wondered when the Allemands would get busy;
And then, of course, they started with five-nines
Traversing, sure as fate, and never a dud.
Mute in the clamour of shells he watched them burst
Spouting dark earth and wire with gusts from hell,
While posturing giants dissolved in drifts of smoke.
He crouched and flinched, dizzy with galloping fear,
Sick for escape,—loathing the strangled horror
And butchered, frantic gestures of the dead.

An officer came blundering down the trench:
"Stand-to and man the fire-step!" On he went . . .
Gasping and bawling, "Fire-step . . . counter-attack!"
    Then the haze lifted. Bombing on the right
    Down the old sap: machine-guns on the left;
    And stumbling figures looming out in front.
    "O Christ, they're coming at us!" Bullets spat,
And he remembered his rifle . . . rapid fire . . .
And started blazing wildly . . . then a bang
Crumpled and spun him sideways, knocked him out
To grunt and wriggle: none heeded him; he choked
And fought the flapping veils of smothering gloom,
Lost in a blurred confusion of yells and groans. . . .
Down, and down, and down, he sank and drowned,
Bleeding to death. The counter-attack had failed.

SIEGFRIED SASSOON

Cows in Red Pasture

Last summer in a Kentish field
I saw the plush green darkened by
A whim of light and darkened too
By whiteness of the sheep which stood
Diminished by the distance so
They looked like gravestones on the green,
So still and small and white they seemed.
As this warm memory blurs and fades,
The emptiness bequeathed instructs
Me, curiously, to resurrect
An older memory of a field
Which I would rather far forget:
A foreign field, a field of France,
In which there lay two cows, one white
With maps of black stamped on its hide,
The other just the colour of
The caramel that I once loved.

Both were still; the toffee one
Lay on its back, its stiff legs stuck
Up from the swollen belly like
A huge discarded set of bagpipes.
The piebald cow lay on its side
Looking like any summer beast
Until one saw it had no head.

The grass on which they lay was red.

VERNON SCANNELL

Autumn

There is a wind where the rose was;
Cold rain where sweet grass was;
        And clouds like sheep
        Stream o'er the steep
Grey skies where the lark was.

Nought gold where your hair was;
Nought warm where your hand was;
        But phantom, forlorn,
        Beneath the thorn,
Your ghost where your face was.

Sad winds where your voice was;
Tears, tears where my heart was;
        And ever with me,
        Child, ever with me,
Silence where hope was.

WALTER DE LA MARE

Is It Far to Go?

Is it far to go?
    A step—no further.

Is it hard to go?
    Ask the melting snow
    The eddying feather.

What can I take there?
    Not a hank, not a hair.

What shall I leave behind?
    Ask the hastening wind,
    The fainting star.

Shall I be gone long?
    For ever and a day.

To whom there belong?
    Ask the stone to say,
    Ask my song.

Who will say farewell?
    The beating bell.

Will anyone miss me?
    That I dare not tell—
    Quick, Rose, and kiss me.

C. DAY LEWIS

Little Boys of Texas

The little boys of Texas prance
To swimming places without their pants
And dive in deep to cool their souls
In very dubious swimming-holes.

The checkered rattlesnake hides there,
He does not ever care to share
His water, slimy as can be,
With any Christian company.

The diamond-back whose single bite
Is full of everlasting night
Lurks beside the sunken log
Short-tempered as a love-crossed dog.

The hoop-snake puts her sharp tail in
Her mouth and rolls as fast as sin
To be at the water bright and smart
With murder at her slender heart.

And there the deadly cotton-mouth,
Honey-mannered as the South,
Lies saying, "You-all sure are sweet!"
And stabs quick death into your feet.

But boys of Texas do not fret
So long's the water there is wet,
They drink in quarts of typhoid fever,
And laugh and yell without a quiver.

They never mind a bitten toe,
These grandsons of the Alamo,
They are as tough as spikes and nails
These Davy Crocketts with hard tails.

And when they leave the slimy bank,
There they lie, stiff, rank on rank,
Cotton-mouth, rattler, hoop, outspread,
Sadder, wiser, and plumb dead.

ROBERT P. TRISTRAM COFFIN

Incidents in the Life of My Uncle Arly

O my agèd Uncle Arly!
Sitting on a heap of Barley
        Thro' the silent hours of night,—
Close beside a leafy thicket:—
On his nose there was a Cricket,—
In his hat a Railway-Ticket;—
        (But his shoes were far too tight).

Long ago, in youth, he squander'd
All his goods away, and wander'd
        To the Tiniskoop-hills afar.
There on golden sunsets blazing,
Every evening found him gazing,—
Singing,—'Orb! you're quite amazing!
        How I wonder what you are!'

Like the ancient Medes and Persians,
Always by his own exertions
        He subsisted on those hills;—
Whiles,—by teaching children spelling,—
Or at times by merely yelling,—
Or at intervals by selling
        'Propter's Nicodemus Pills.'

Later, in his morning rambles
He perceived the moving brambles—
        Something square and white disclose;—
'Twas a First-class Railway-Ticket;
But, on stooping down to pick it
Off the ground,—a pea-green Cricket
        Settled on my uncle's Nose.

Never—never more,—oh! never,
Did that Cricket leave him ever,—
        Dawn or evening, day or night;—
Clinging as a constant treasure,—
Chirping with a cheerious measure,—
Wholly to my uncle's pleasure,—
        ('Though his shoes were far too tight).

So for three-and-forty winters,
Till his shoes were worn to splinters,
        All those hills he wander'd o'er,—
Sometimes silent;—sometimes yelling;—
Till he came to Borley-Melling,
Near his old ancestral dwelling;—
        (But his shoes were far too tight).

On a little heap of Barley
Died my agèd Uncle Arly,
        And they buried him one night;—
Close beside the leafy thicket:—
There,—his hat and Railway-Ticket;—
There,—his ever-faithful Cricket;—
        (But his shoes were far too tight).

EDWARD LEAR

The Dancing Cabman

Alone on the lawn
  The cabman dances;
In the dew of the dawn
  He kicks and prances.
His bowler is set
  On his bullet-head.
For his boots are wet
  And his aunt is dead.
There on the lawn
  As the light advances,
On the tide of the dawn,
  The cabman dances.

Swift and strong
  As a garden roller,
He dances along
  In his little bowler,
Skimming the lawn
  With royal grace,
The dew of the dawn
  On his great red face.
To fairy flutes,
  As the light advances,
In square, black boots
  The cabman dances.

J. B. MORTON

Jabberwocky

'Twas brillig, and the slithy toves
  Did gyre and gimble in the wabe:
All mimsy were the borogoves,
  And the mome raths outgrabe.

"Beware the Jabberwock, my son!
    The jaws that bite, the claws that catch!
Beware the Jubjub bird, and shun
    The frumious Bandersnatch!"

He took his vorpal sword in hand;
    Long time the manxome foe he sought—
So rested he by the Tumtum tree,
    And stood awhile in thought.

And, as in uffish thought he stood,
    The Jabberwock, with eyes of flame,
Came whiffling through the tulgey wood,
    And burbled as it came!

One, two! One, two! And through and through
    The vorpal blade went snicker-snack!
He left it dead, and with its head
    He went galumphing back.

"And hast thou slain the Jabberwock?
    Come to my arms, my beamish boy!
O frabjous day! Callooh, Callay!"
    He chortled in his joy.

'Twas brillig, and the slithy toves
    Did gyre and gimble in the wabe:
All mimsy were the borogoves,
    And the mome raths outgrabe.

LEWIS CARROLL

Romance

When I was but thirteen or so
    I went into a golden land,
Chimborazo, Cotopaxi
    Took me by the hand.

My father died, my brother too,
    They passed like fleeting dreams.
I stood where Popocatepetl
    In the sunlight gleams.

I dimly heard the Master's voice
    And boys far-off at play,
Chimborazo, Cotopaxi
    Had stolen me away.

I walked in a great golden dream
    To and fro from school—
Shining Popocatepetl
    The dusty streets did rule.

I walked home with a gold dark boy
    And never a word I'd say,
Chimborazo, Cotopaxi
    Had taken my speech away:

I gazed entranced upon his face
    Fairer than any flower—
O shining Popocatepetl
    It was thy magic hour:

The houses, people, traffic seemed
    Thin fading dreams by day,
Chimborazo, Cotopaxi
    They had stolen my soul away!

WALTER JAMES TURNER

The Song of Wandering Aengus

I went out to the hazel wood,
Because a fire was in my head,
And cut and peeled a hazel wand,
And hooked a berry to a thread;
And when white moths were on the wing,
And moth-like stars were flickering out,
I dropped the berry in a stream,
And caught a little silver trout.

When I had laid it on the floor
I went to blow the fire aflame,
But something rustled on the floor,
And someone called me by my name;
It had become a glimmering girl
With apple blossom in her hair
Who called me by my name and ran
And faded through the brightening air.

Though I am old with wandering
Through hollow lands and hilly lands,
I will find out where she has gone,
And kiss her lips and take her hands;
And walk among long dappled grass,
And pluck till time and times are done
The silver apples of the moon,
The golden apples of the sun.

W. B. YEATS

The Sisters

We were two daughters of one race:
She was the fairest in the face:
  The wind is blowing in turret and tree.
They were together, and she fell;
Therefore revenge became me well.
  O the Earl was fair to see!

She died: she went to burning flame:
She mix'd her ancient blood with shame.
  The wind is howling in turret and tree.
Whole weeks and months, and early and late,
To win his love I lay in wait:
  O the Earl was fair to see!

I made a feast; I bad him come;
I won his love, I brought him home.
  The wind is roaring in turret and tree.
And after supper, on a bed,
Upon my lap he laid his head:
  O the Earl was fair to see!

I kiss'd his eyelids into rest:
His ruddy cheek upon my breast.
  The wind is raging in turret and tree.
I hated him with the hate of hell,
But I loved his beauty passing well.
  O the Earl was fair to see!

I rose up in the silent night:
I made my dagger sharp and bright.
  The wind is raving in turret and tree.
As half-asleep his breath he drew,
Three times I stabbed him thro' and thro'.
  O the Earl was fair to see!

I curl'd and com'b his comely head,
He look'd so grand when he was dead.
    The wind is blowing in turret and tree.
I wrapt his body in the sheet,
And laid him at his mother's feet.
    O the Earl was fair to see!

ALFRED, LORD TENNYSON

Old Christmas

"Where are you coming from, Lomey Carter,
    So airly over the snow?
And what's them pretties you got in your hand,
    And where you aiming to go?

"Step in, Honey: Old Christmas morning
    I ain't got nothing much;
Maybe a bite of sweetness and corn bread,
    A little ham meat and such.

"But come in, Honey! Sally Anne Barton's
    Hungering after your face.
Wait till I light my candle up:
    Set down! There's your old place.

"Now where you been so airly this morning?"
    "Graveyard, Sally Anne.
Up by the trace in the salt lick meadows
    Where Taulbe kilt my man."

"Taulbe ain't to home this morning . . .
    I can't scratch up a light:
Dampness gets on the heads of the matches;
    But I'll blow up the embers bright."

"Needn't trouble. I won't be stopping:
Going a long ways still."
"You didn't see nothing, Lomey Carter,
Up on the graveyard hill?"

"What should I see there, Sally Anne Barton?"
"Well, sperits do walk last night."
"There were an elder bush a-blooming
While the moon still gave some light."

"Yes, elder bushes, they bloom, Old Christmas,
And critters kneel down in their straw.
Anything else up in the graveyard?"
"One thing more I saw:

"I saw my man with his head all bleeding
Where Taulbe's shot went through."
"What did he say?" *"He stooped and kissed me."*
"What did he say to you?"

"Said, Lord Jesus forguv your Taulbe;
But he told me another word;
He said it soft when he stooped and kissed me.
That were the last I heard."

"Taulbe ain't to home this morning."
"I know that, Sally Anne,
For I kilt him, coming down through the meadow
Where Taulbe kilt my man.

"I met him upon the meadow trace
When the moon were fainting fast,
And I had my dead man's rifle gun
And kilt him as he come past."

"But I heard two shots." *"'Twas his was second:*
He shot me 'fore he died:
You'll find us at daybreak, Sally Anne Barton:
I'm laying there dead at his side."

ROY HELTON

Flight of the Roller Coaster

Once more around should do it, the man confided . . .

and sure enough, when the roller-coaster reached the peak
of the giant curve above me, screech of its wheels
almost drowned out by the shriller cries of the riders,

instead of the dip and plunge with its landslide of screams,
it rose in the air like a movieland magic carpet,
some wonderful bird,
and without fuss or fanfare swooped slowly across
the amusement park,
over Spook's Castle, ice-cream booths, shooting-gallery.
And losing no height

made the last yards above the beach, where the cucumber-cool
brakeman in the last seat saluted
a lady about to change from her bathing-suit.

Then, as many witnesses reported, headed leisurely
out over the water,
disappearing all too soon behind a low-flying flight of clouds.

RAYMOND SOUSTER

A Green Lowland of Pianos

in the evening
as far as the eye can see
herds
of black pianos

up to their knees
in the mire
they listen to the frogs

they gurgle in water
with chords of rapture

they are entranced
by froggish, moonish spontaneity

after the vacation
they cause scandals
in a concert hall
during the artistic milking
suddenly they lie down
like cows

looking with indifference
at the white flowers
of the audience

at the gesticulating
of the ushers

JERZY HARASYMOWICZ
(from the Polish)

Goodbat Nightman

God bless all policemen
and fighters of crime,
May thieves go to jail
for a very long time.

They've had a hard day
helping clean up the town,
Now they hang from the mantelpiece
both upside down.

A glass of warm blood
and then straight up the stairs,
Batman and Robin
are saying their prayers.

They've locked all the doors
and they've put out the bat,
Put on their batjamas
(They like doing that)

They've filled their batwater-bottles
made their batbeds,
With two springy battresses
for sleepy batheads.

They're closing red eyes
and they're counting black sheep,
Batman and Robin
are falling asleep.

ROGER MCGOUGH

NOTES

P. 57 Armadale Avenue Revisited

Stutz Touring: an early automobile

P. 59 Snow in the Suburbs

palings: the boards of a picket fence

inurn: bury, entomb

nether: lower

blanched: whitened

P. 61 Hot Cake

rheum: mucus

lackeys: servants

P. 65 Klaxon

klaxon: a very powerful horn sometimes used in automobiles. Its use is generally illegal because of its extreme blast of noise.

P. 66 We Are Going to See the Rabbit

hoarding: display board for advertisements

underground: subway train

motorway: large main highway

P. 68 Chanson Innocent

goat-footed: In the second part of the poem the balloon man is seen, not as lame, but as 'goat-footed.' The Greeks and Romans imagined the forest gods as being half man and half goat. They called these gods *satyrs.* The most famous of these creatures was the god *Pan*, god of Nature, who gave his name to the wind instrument called *Panpipes.* Cummings imagines the whistling balloon man to be the god Pan returning to celebrate the spring.

P. 69 Factory Windows

Yahoo: an allusion to Swift's *Gulliver's Travels.* The yahoos were vicious brutes in human form who were the servants of the gentle *Houyhnhnms,* horses possessed of human reason. The word yahoo is now generally used to mean brutish or degraded people.

derisive: mocking

Denmark: an allusion to the play *Hamlet* by Shakespeare. The line has the general meaning that factory work is degrading. Lindsay is expressing in this poem a radical criticism of industrialized society. He sees factories as the outward signs of the exploitation of the people and deplores a system whose effect is to dehumanize and degrade.

P. 70 Ghostly Story

Clydesdale: an extremely large and stately horse formerly used for hauling heavy wagons

P. 72 The Miller

stone: English measure of weight. One stone is equal to fourteen pounds.

ram: a sheep put up for the prize

buckler: shield

wrangler: he loved loud arguments

buffoon: teller of coarse jokes and stories, a clown

took three times his due: he was paid for grinding corn with a percentage of the flour

P. 73 Alison

sloes: a blue-black wild plum

wether: a male sheep

girdle: ornamental belt

florin: a gold coin

rick: a stack of hay

mead: an alcoholic drink made from honey

boss: a round metal ornament at the centre of a shield

P. 74 The Summoner

summoner: an official of the Church concerned with the enforcement of Church law and morality

cherubinny: cherubs were child-like angels who were usually portrayed as having great, swelling cheeks

quicksilver etc.: substances used for their medicinal effect

brimstone: sulphur

salve: an ointment

whelks: pustules; that is, his over-ripe carbuncles

purge: to cleanse or purify

P. 78 Mrs. Reece Laughs

stays: the whale bone supports in an old-fashioned corset or girdle

P. 79 Mrs. Ogmore-Pritchard

The passage represents her dreams.

linoleum, retired: a retired salesman of linoleum

besoming: sweeping with a *besom* or broom

balsam: medicine

P. 83 The Centurion

colonnades: a row of columns supporting a roof. A colonnade ran round the sides of the town square and provided a shaded place in which to sit or walk.

purple: a colour reserved in the Roman world for emperors

seamless: See St. John 19: 23-24

P. 85 Butch Weldy

fellow-servant: Butch Weldy has been cheated out of any compensation on the technicality that the accident was caused by the negligence of a fellow-servant and not by the negligence of the company (Old Rhodes' son) employing him.

P. 88 Levy Silver

Rhinestones: artificial gems made of glass or paste

synthetic: imitation

gold-filled: gold plated

spurious: fake or pretended

P. 91 Farm Scene

blathering: the silly noises made by the bellowing calves

fothered: herded together

lap: bank the fire up for the night

P. 92 Digging

bracken: ferns

P. 93 Tall Nettles

elm butt: a barrel made of elm to hold rain water

P. 96 A Sheep Fair

ewes: female sheep

mewed: penned in, imprisoned

P. 97 Moonlit Apples

wainscot: panelling

tryst: a romantic meeting

P. 98 Pied Beauty

brinded cow: brown cow marked with darker patches and blotches

stipple: dots

trim: equipment

fold, fallow, and plough: the way the plots and pieces of land are being used. Some is used for grazing, some is lying idle, and some is ploughed.

fathers-forth: God 'fathers-forth,' or is the originator of, all this beauty

P. 101 The Heron

antic: ludicrous

P. 101 The Fish

isinglass: mica. A thin transparent material which was formerly used in automobile windows. Mica quickly stains and runs with a network of tiny cracks.

P. 104 Mountain Lion

¿Qué tiene, amigo?: (Spanish) What have you got there, friend?

Hermoso es: It's beautiful

Sangre de Christo: Blood of Christ

P. 110 Snake

Etna: a volcano in Sicily

paltry: worthless, contemptible

albatross: an extremely large seabird. The reference is to Coleridge's "The Rime of the Ancient Mariner." The mariner shot an albatross for no good reason and was put under a curse for this thoughtless act.

expiate: to make atonement for sin

P. 114 The Best Beast

lift: elevator

P. 118 Cargoes

Quinquireme: a ship rowed by five banks of oars
Nineveh: a city in ancient Assyria
Ohpir: mentioned in the Bible as a land rich in gold

apes: a great rarity and curiosity in the ancient world

sandalwood and cedarwood: prized because of their beautiful smell

Isthmus: the Isthmus of Panama

cinnamon: a then valuable spice

moidores: a gold coin of Portugal or Brazil

pig-lead: lead in pigs or blocks

P. 118 Old Song Re-sung

silver call: bosun's pipe or whistle

brails: ropes attached to sails

spirit-room: paymaster's store room where the rum and wine was kept under lock and key

P. 122 Eight Haiku

The haiku is a poetic form traditional to Japan. It must have three lines of five, seven and five syllables respectively. The strict rules governing the form are difficult to follow in translation and many translations are only an approximation of the original. The haiku is still extremely popular in Japan and annual competitions are judged by the Emperor.

P. 126 The Two Corbies

corbies: carrion crows

P. 127 The Leaden Echo

Attention in reading this poem should be paid not to meaning, which is simple, but to the patterns of sound. The poem plays variations on the question, "Is there no way of keeping beauty from vanishing?" The poem *must* be read aloud. Experiment with it.

P. 129 Bombing Casualties in Spain

bleb: here meaning the lip

P. 129. Giorno Dei Morti: (Italian) The Day of the Dead

surplices: a white linen garment worn over the cloaks

P. 133 All that's Past

brier: a wild rose bush

amaranth: the name given to an imaginary flower which never fades. A symbol of immortality

P. 137 Captain Cat

The passage represents the dreams of the retired sea captain.

donkeyman: a man who runs a small steam engine called a donkey *sea-lawyer:* meaning much the same as 'barrack-room lawyer'—argumentative

Mumbles: a place in South Wales

ormolu: gilded bronze

laverbread: a type of seaweed eaten as relish

Ebenezer's bell: the bell of the Methodist chapel

tiddlers: minnows

whippets: dogs rather like greyhounds used for hunting rabbits and hares

snug: the parlour of a public-house

Dowlais: South Wales (pronounced *Dowlice*—emphasis on first syllable)

Maesgwyn: South Wales (pronounced Mice-gwin—emphasis on second syllable)

P. 140 Dulce Et Decorum Est

froth-corrupted lungs: lungs broken down by the acid gas

cud of vile, incurable sores: sores caused by the burning gas. Owen is contrasting *innocent tongues* with the tongues which tell the *Old Lie.*

Dulce et decorum est pro patria mori: a Latin tag meaning: It is sweet and fitting to die for one's country.

P. 141 Acquainted with the Night

Do lines one and fourteen mean the same thing?

P. 141 O What Is that Sound?

This poem does not seem to make much sense if you read it as a narrative because it does not tell you *why* the soldiers are coming or *why* they wish to capture or kill the young man. We might even say that pointlessness is the point of the poem. It is concerned with sudden and inexplicable violence and nightmare terror. Perhaps Auden was trying to express, in metaphorical terms, what it was like for the ordinary person to live in Hitler's Germany or Franco's Spain. You might bring the poem politically up to date by substituting Vietnam, the Congo, or the Middle East for Germany and Spain.

Note to the Teacher

This poem is similar to many surrealistic poems that Auden wrote in the Thirties. These poems present pictures and images which are imaginative parallels of the violence and terror of the times. (e.g. Epilogue to "The Orators" (1932); "Something Is Bound to Happen" (1930); "As I Walked Out One Evening" (1940)). It is possible to isolate certain stanzas from the last mentioned poem which illuminate the technique and theme of "O What Is that Sound?"

P. 143 Counter-attack

Lewis guns: machine guns

five-nines: a large shell or the gun which fires such shells

sap: an extension from a trench dug towards the enemy's position

P. 152 Romance

Chimborazo and Cotopaxi: peaks in the South American Andes

Popocatepetl: a dormant volcano in Mexico

P. 153 The Song of Wandering Aengus

Aengus: in Irish mythology the god of love and beauty. The fisherman in the poem need not, however, be identified with the god.

P. 155 Old Christmas

trace: path

salt-lick: where cattle gather to lick salt which occurs naturally on the surface of the earth

P. 159 Goodbat Nightman

Part of this poem's humour is based on its similarity to A. A. Milne's poem about Christopher Robin saying his prayers.

TITLE INDEX

AUTHOR INDEX